The places described in this book are accessible today from three major entry points: Minnewaska State Park, Sam's Point (via Cragsmoor) and Ellenville, all in the Shawangunk Mountains.

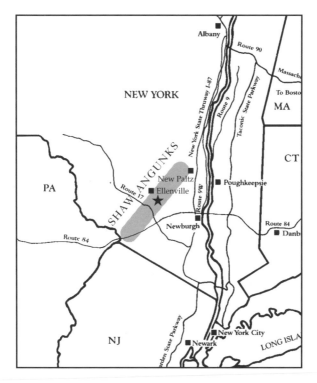

★ The star corresponds to the huckleberry pickers' territory depicted in detail on the next page. *Courtesy of Mohonk Mountain House.*

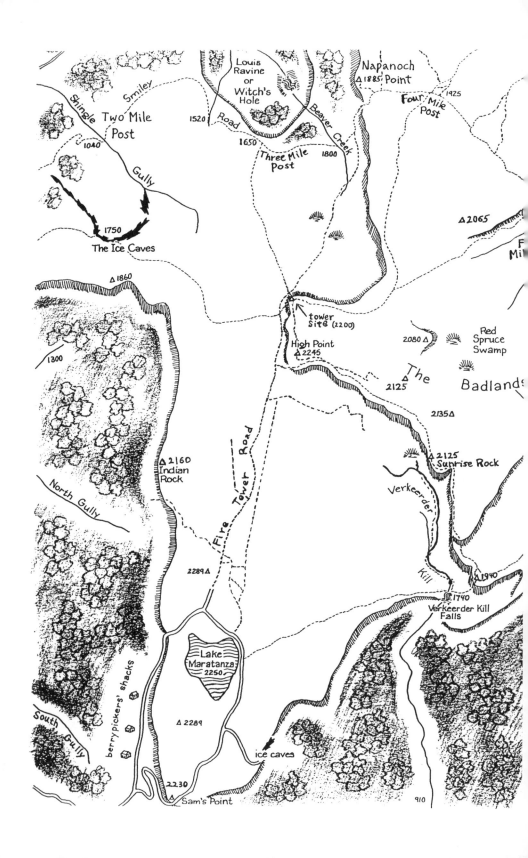

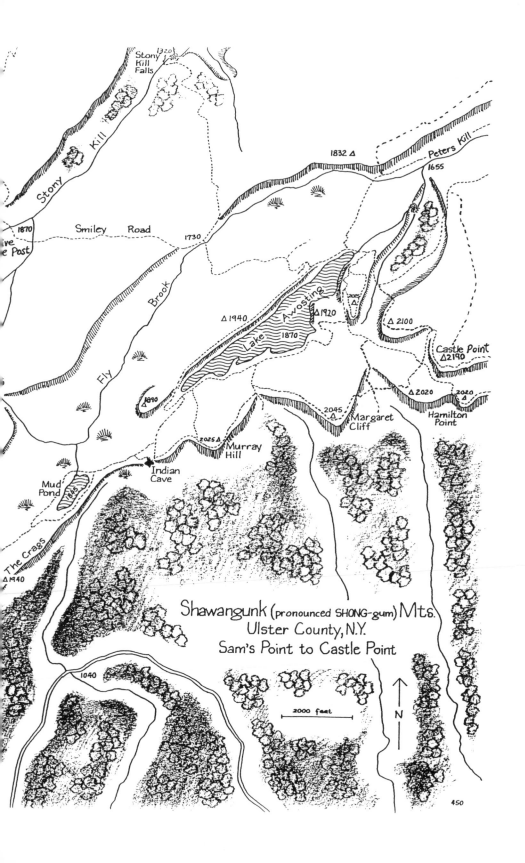

Shawangunk (pronounced SHONG-gum) Mts.
Ulster County, N.Y.
Sam's Point to Castle Point

2000 feet

N

450

The
Huckleberry Pickers

A Raucous History
OF THE
Shawangunk Mountains

Marc B. Fried

BLACK DOME PRESS CORP
RR 1, Box 422
Hensonville, NY 12439
Tel: (518) 734-6357
Fax: (518) 734-5802

Published by

Black Dome Press Corp.
RR1, Box 422
Hensonville, New York 12439
(518) 734-6357

First Edition, 1995
Second Printing, 1998

Library of Congress Cataloging-in-Publication Data
Fried, Marc B.
    The Huckleberry Pickers: a raucous history of the
Shawangunk mountains/Marc B. Fried.—1st ed.
        p. cm.
    ISBN 1-883789-04-4
    1. Shawangunk Mountains (N.Y.)—Social life and customs.
2. Agricultural laborers—New York (State)—Shawangunk
Mountains—History. I. Title.
F127.U4F76   1995
974.7'31—dc20   95-10289
                                                                CIP

Book Design by Artemisia, Inc.
Printed in the USA

When *Tales from the Shawangunk Mountains* was published in January 1982, I gave Nina Addis a copy in which I made an inscription. It often occurred to me later that what I wrote in Nina's book could as appropriately have served as a dedication, or indeed as an epitaph, and that the sentiment I expressed to Nina applies in many respects to Lillian Crawford Wood; to Blacky and Meinrad; to Fred Conklin; and perhaps to Mary Crose, the talented Bill Countryman, and many other Shawangunk berrypickers whom I never had the good fortune to meet in person:

> *You are part of the history of the Shawangunk Mountains. And you have made history in the best possible way: by simply taking part in life's adventure, enduring its hardships, joining in laughter at its follies, and most importantly, in being sensitive to its beauties.*

It is to the many whom these words describe that this book is affectionately dedicated.

$\mathcal{C}$ontents

Foreword

When Marc Fried first visited my office at the Carl Carmer Center for Catskill Mountain and Hudson River Studies, at SUNY New Paltz, I was fascinated by what he had to say about the berrypickers of the Shawangunks, compelled by his knowledge of and enthusiasm for the subject, and, I must here confess, somewhat skeptical regarding the enterprise of making a book centered on that topic. How misplaced that jot of skepticism was! I was familiar with Mr. Fried's fine, scholarly work on seventeenth-century Ulster County, but I had no inkling, at the time, of the depth of Fried's engagement with his terrain, his autochthonous connection with every aspect of his subject, his passionate topophilia, and his writerly craft—both scholarly and creative—which he deploys so effectively in this volume. Here he makes a place, a unique intersection of land and history and people, come vividly alive.

On that first day we talked, I tried to steer Mr. Fried to whatever might be useful in the Norman Studer Regional Archives. I told him about a song (which he includes here), "Huckleberry Bill," which Studer had collected from a Shawangunk berrypicker he interviewed during the Camp Woodland days. Since I sometimes give concerts of regional folk music, and since it's not easy to find a Shawangunk folksong, I had taken to singing a version of "Huckleberry Bill" at various performances in this region. Little did I suspect that such a simple song—one that I reckon I sang, in part, because of fond memories it evoked of the days when I picked blueberries as a migrant laborer, thirty-some years ago—would open the door, for me, to the rich and intricate "huckleberry history" that this book unfolds. From Fried's valuable research, I now know a good deal more about the sources of that song and about all the folk traditions of the Shawangunk Mountains.

Any lingering doubt I may have harbored about the aptness of the berrypickers' world as a point of entry to the mysteries of place vanished when Fried spoke to my graduate seminar in the Literature and Lore of the Hudson Valley. In an address of less than an hour's duration, he made the secret, lost world of the Shawangunk berrypicker and the very mountains themselves come intensely alive for that class. He provided a valuable touchstone for that numinous sense of place to which some of us still attach the highest value, near the end of a century that has all but abandoned such knowledge. In a series of visiting speakers that included distinguished scholars of various aspects of Hudson Valley lore and history, Mr. Fried's presentation was remarkable for its poised yet rapt possession of the very thing, always elusive and indefinable, that I was attempting to cultivate in those students.

Thus it was that when Mr. Fried called to ask if I would read through the manuscript of this book, I immediately said yes. I said yes in spite of a crowded calendar of my own writing deadlines, in spite of three books on my own desk begging to be finished. And I count myself fortunate in having said yes, as any reader of this book will, for here we enter truly and deeply into a place, and we come away with something rare and compelling.

For the student of history and folklore, this is an invaluable record: Fried has recorded the colorful storytelling of generations of berrypickers before they vanish forever from the face of the Shawangunk earth. And he has let them have their say, without the intrusive and deadening jargon of some folklorists and historians. The author lingers over the flavor of all this (as will the reader) with affection, but without a trace of that diminishing tone of sentimentality or condescension that is so often imported into this kind of place-writing. Fried's writing reminds us of the gifts of the great narrators and narratives of place, the Faulkners and the Yoknapatawpha Counties: Let the people who lived it talk, and let us listen to their voices; let the land speak, and let us listen to what the land is saying. Fried admirably realizes this design.

With this volume, Fried takes his place among those writers who have known that it is better to have, to truly possess, one place, so that we may better know and have all places. In the bright particularity of the berrypickers' experience, in an obscure nook of rural New York State, shimmers the entire universe, the burden of human experience, and the tremulous web of Nature.

H. R. Stoneback
Professor of American Literature,
Director, Carl Carmer Center for
Catskill Mountain & Hudson River Studies,
SUNY New Paltz

Preface

Since the publication of *Tales from the Shawangunk Mountains*, a wealth of new material has come my way concerning the mountain's indigenous berrypicking communities. A picture has emerged of a unique subculture that for nearly a century profoundly influenced the economic and social life of the Shawangunk region, until disappearing scarcely more than a generation ago.

Significant commerce in wild huckleberries from the Shawangunks is on record as early as 1862. Other Shawangunk Mountain industries of the nineteenth century included the cutting of cordwood and timber, and the harvest of hemlock bark for tanning leather; the manufacture of wooden shingles, barrel hoops, and charcoal; and the hewing of millstones and mining of lead and zinc ores from the stone of the northwestern slopes.

Huckleberrying was the last survivor among these native industries linked intimately and tangibly to the mountain's physical resources. Each summer the Shawangunks became home to hundreds of pickers, who pitched their tents or built their tarpaper shanties amid the rock slabs and pine barrens or in the shadow of the summit escarpment. Many discovered here a profound sense of community; for some, the mountain itself became almost personified and left upon their lives an indelible impression.

The stories told to me by those whose formative years were shaped in this rustic environment are often poignant and highly revealing—at other times, scandalously entertaining. In combining oral sources with documentary research, I have attempted to transcend the merely anecdotal and present a meaningful biographical context for the personalities and events described. If I've succeeded, it is in large part through the inspiration, friendship, and cooperation I have experienced among the subjects of these studies, as well as the curiosity instilled in me, by the living, for those who died before my time.

In putting the results of my research into literary form, I faced the dilemma of writing for two different audiences: those who have read my previous book and those who are new to the subject. My task was to create a narrative that would stand on its own without resorting to introductory or explanatory material that would prove repetitious for my past readers. Ultimately, though it is hardly a prerequisite, familiarity with the contents of my earlier work can not help but enhance the reader's understanding of the present one. (For instance, because the story of Nina Addis is already told to substantial degree in *Tales*, this remarkable personage, since deceased, is accorded a somewhat less prominent position herein.)

A word about methodology: The greater part of the historical material contained in this book is based on oral sources, usually identified or inferable. In a very few instances, a source has been kept anonymous for reasons of discretion. Wherever possible, I've attempted to verify or augment the recollections of one person with those of others and with documentary material, and thus to present a composite that seems faithful to the sum of credible evidence. Unless otherwise noted, quoted oral statements of any length are derived from tape recordings in my possession. While some editing of such spontaneous conversation is often unavoidable, I have rigorously steered clear of rendering the language more picturesque or idiosyncratic than in the original.

Genealogical material and personal data contained in this book are based on personal records or recollections of individuals; vital statistics maintained by the registrars of local municipalities; tombstone inscriptions derived from my own visits to cemeteries or from Poucher and Terwilliger's *Old Gravestones of Ulster County*; and on the records kept by a local funeral home. For biographical information relating to land ownership I have consulted the deed records for Ulster and Sullivan counties in the offices of the respective county clerks.

Every person named in this book who has told me of his or her experiences in the Shawangunk Mountains is owed a debt of gratitude by me, and as well by my readers; in a very real sense, these individuals are coauthors of a joint venture. But I can hardly do justice to the help and cooperation provided me without special mention of two people whose input went well beyond personal reminiscences to include extensive recollections concerning people and events of which they were themselves observers. To Bernard ("Hype") Addis, son of the illustrious Nina, and to Lillian Crawford Wood, special appreciation and thanks are therefore due.

Prior to publication, the manuscript was read by Professor H. R. Stoneback of SUNY New Paltz, by my brother Robert L. Fried, Associate Professor of Education, University of Hartford, and by Donald R. Friary, Executive Director and Secretary, Historic Deerfield, Inc. (Massachusetts), all of whom offered valuable criticism and encouragement. I would also like to acknowledge Patricia H. Davis and Matina Billias for their careful copyediting.

PART I

The Smiley Road Revisited

Chapter 1

Ellenville
to the Two-Mile Post

*Since last year a new road of easy grades,
seven miles long, has been constructed—
running all the way through a wild, uncultivated
country—from Awosting Lake to a railroad station at
Ellenville. Much of this road is strikingly grand and
beautiful.*

So wrote Mr. Alfred H. Smiley in 1901, in the annual
brochure for the Minnewaska Mountain Houses, of which he
was proprietor. Some of the folks who came up from the
Ellenville side to pick huckleberries along this right-of-way
called it the New Road. This name was still preferred eighty
years after the road's construction by one former berrypicker I
talked to, Lou Quick of Walden. But the name that was more
commonly used and that eventually stuck was one
acknowledging the builder: the Smiley Road. Of the many who
were employed as laborers during construction of the road, I
know the actual identity of only two persons. One was William
Fahy, Sr., father of the elderly William Fahy, late of Ellenville.
The other was Nina Addis's father, Albert Quick, who was a
teenager at the time. Nina's son Bernie ("Hype") Addis
remembers hearing that wages were "a dollar a day, and if you
stopped to light your pipe you was fired."

Turning from Canal Street onto the narrow side-road called Mine Lane, we enter a large, weedy meadow, site of the old Ellenville dump, and immediately our attention is drawn to a tall, narrow opening in the bedrock at the foot of Shawangunk Mountain. This is the entrance to the Ellenville Mine, whose magnificent quartz crystals have long graced glass-front displays at the State Museum in Albany and in New York's Museum of Natural History. Years ago, as I understand it, the Village fathers, mindful of possible hazards such an irresistible attraction posed to curious Ellenville youths, but also ever sensitive to the historical and geological significance of this ancient mine hole, solved their predicament with wondrous imagination by dumping a truckload of fill into the opening.

We head northeastward across the flats, keeping close to the base of the mountain, and in a few minutes arrive at the starting point of our day's outing: the rocky old roadbed that will carry us up the mountain on our seven-mile journey. Our route will take us past clear mountain brooks, through shady forests, and high across desolate pine barrens to Lake Awosting, a jewel of sparkling waters set amongst white cliffs near the crest of the Shawangunk range.

The Smiley Road starts gamely along up the mountain and then, as if losing its nerve, almost immediately makes a sharp hairpin turn to the right; then a second hairpin back to the left, like a rabbit attempting to throw us off scent. Satisfied that we mean to persist in seeking its company and unlocking its secrets, it digs in for the long haul and becomes a bit more hospitable, leading us at a moderate but steady grade on our journey eastward. A bit of badly disintegrating asphalt clings to the roadbed here and there, where floodwaters have not yet succeeded in carrying all the pavement down the mountainside. I am told this improvement to the lowermost portion of the road was done many years ago by Ellenville as an accommodation to Village employees, who were permitted to cut firewood here for their own use.

A little beyond the last remnant of pavement, on the right-hand side of the road, we come to a flat shelf of rock that was known as the Resting Rock to the folks who camped at the Two-Mile Post, some of whom often made the trip to and from Ellenville on foot. Fred Conklin, who lived on Berme Road outside Ellenville, told me that about the early 1950s he and his brother George once secreted a half-gallon bottle of wine under a rock near here, below the roadbed on the downhill side. They had started up the mountain with two bottles, and the one that didn't get hidden under the rock served to blur their recollection concerning the exact whereabouts of the one that did. When they returned sometime later, they could not locate the bottle despite a desperate search. Fred was sure the jug lay hidden there still; perhaps some lucky soul may yet find it.

About twelve to fifteen minutes from the bottom of the mountain, the road bends rightward around a steep slab of encroaching bedrock and enters a little hollow, before recurving to the left. Fred told me a reliable stream of water formerly flowed off the rocks here. The exposed bedrock is fractured and faulted, apparently from the same gravitational slippage that created the vast array of fissures and ice-filled crevices higher up on the mountainside.

This spot was known as the One-Mile Post, though the presence of berrypickers in this vicinity was never more than minimal. On the right-hand side of the road, at two locations a little below and above this spot, there are flat areas where pickers occasionally camped in the back of a truck or in tents, until perhaps the early forties. Directly across from the lower of these two places, on the opposite side of the road, there is a large flat area below the roadbed where a shanty once stood. This was accessible by motor vehicle via a driveway of sorts that is still vaguely discernible where it enters the Smiley Road yet a little farther down.

We continue on our trek eastward and soon come to a stretch of the road worthy of note principally for some vehicular mishaps that occurred within a relatively short distance of one another: About the early 1940s, the declivity to our left ate a '38

Chevy being driven up the mountain by George Conklin. The car was loaded with beer, wine, liquor, and Conklin kin. It rolled over three or four times before coming to rest by a tree, and a little girl who "flew out the side-door winnder" was miraculously protected, as the car rolled over top of her, supposedly by a large dent in the roof caused when the car had landed on a rock during its previous time around a moment earlier. All this according to the recollection of George Conklin's son Fred, previously referred to, who was about seven or eight years old at the time. The electric company came up the mountain with a power winch, which they attached to a tree farther up the slope, and eventually hoisted the vehicle back up onto the road. "Meantime, when they was takin' the cable up there to hook onto the tree, there was a hornets' nest up in there," Fred told me. "I said to my brother I said 'Let's have some fun.' He just about got to that hornets' nest and I fired this rock. It hit the hornets' nest and. . . I mean it's not funny, but I did it. Boy, that guy he let go of the cable and he was hauling down that bank."

A man driving a panel truck also once went over the edge—but didn't roll over—at a point perhaps several hundred feet lower down along the road, about two minutes by foot above the One-Mile Post. This may have been the berrypicker known as "Boston Blacky," not to be confused with the Blacky whose story is told in chapter 4. He was traveling up the mountain more than a little too fast for his condition at the time, which Fred said was similar to his father's condition when *he'd* gone over the edge. Fred and his brother George, their mother, Mildred, and aunt Rose, and a canine companion, were in the panel truck at the time of the mishap. Rose opened the door with a screwdriver (the door handle was broken or missing) when the man's driving became worrisome, and they all jumped out the back of the truck an instant before it left the road. About 1956 or '57 Fred himself went over the edge, in between these other two locations, and got stuck; the car was pulled out a few days later by a man with a La Salle automobile who had made it all the way up to the Four-Mile Post, despite the deteriorated condition of the road by then, and who helped Fred get his car out on the way back down.

Several minutes farther east we come to a small loop in the road, with a rock "island" in the middle. The original roadbed lay to the right of this island; the left-hand detour was necessitated by a severe washout from the August 1955 flood. We come to a sharp, rightward horseshoe turn and then an even sharper curve to the left, a short distance above. At the point of this second horseshoe, just off the edge of the road to the right, is a U.S. Coast and Geodetic Survey marker bearing the date 1942. Leaving the road for a moment, we'll climb down a few paces to get a look at the massive man-made stone wall upon which this switchback rests.

The road swings rightward as it approaches Shingle Gully, which it crosses on a wooden bridge at the head of a sizeable ravine. The volume of water passing under the bridge is nil, except during times of heavy rain or snowmelt, for most of the flow bypasses the bridge by means of natural fissures higher up in the streambed. This water crosses the road a little beyond the bridge before rejoining the gully. The sides of the ravine are lined with a luxurious growth of rhododendron. This is the only bridge still crossed by the Smiley Road on its trip to Lake Awosting. During the 1955 flood, which was the aftermath of Hurricane Diane, the water was reportedly raging knee-deep over the bridge's roadbed.

I asked Fred Conklin about his memory of the flood: "We was caught in it, we had cars up there," he told me. "The road had great big huge ruts. Some of them you could stand in, it was over your head. But after the flood, somebody had filled in with rocks or made little cuts around the road, but a lot of that had filled back in on its own somehow, from the rains and stuff." The night of the flood, Fred and his brother Danny were down in Ellenville, working the graveyard shift at Channel Master. When they'd driven down the mountain from the Two-Mile Post, they'd left Fred's unregistered '47 Nash at the bottom of the Smiley Road, thinking to return up the mountain the next morning. "So I get to where I left my car, I didn't see no car. That's how bad it sunk down in the ground, it washed out around it so bad that the water was goin' right over the roof of it. We took shovels and picks and made a ramp and pulled it up out of there. Of course it was no good after that anymore. I had to give it to the junkyard."

A couple of minutes up the road from the Shingle Gully bridge, we come to the site of the Two-Mile Post. Fred told me of having spent every summer of his life on the Smiley Road through about the summer of 1964. Born in December 1934, he retained only faint, uncertain memories of the Three-Mile Post, where his family camped prior to the breakup of the berrypicking community there by the State. Thereafter his family and many others from the Three-Mile moved down here to the Two-Mile Post.

From information provided by Fred and by his father's sister Rose, and from the cemetery of the Brick Church (West New Hempstead Reformed Church) near Spring Valley, New York, I have pieced together a most interesting family tree: Fred's mother was Mildred Conklin, the daughter of Thomas "Sherman" Conklin and Minnie Youmans. Minnie's mother was Addie Youmans, who married Abe Youmans (no known relation). Addie's father was Joseph Jonah Youmans, a Civil War veteran, who, by a later marriage, bore a daughter Alice, who married one John ("Jack") Granger Conklin (no known relation to Sherman Conklin). Four of the couple's children were: George, Rose, Julia, and Elsie Conklin. George was Fred Conklin's father, and Fred's mother, Mildred, thus bore the same last name after marriage as before; Rose married Mildred's brother Kenneth and likewise kept the same surname (by a later marriage she became Rose Conklin Hogencamp); George and Rose's sister Julia Conklin married Jesse, who was another brother of Mildred Conklin's; and Elsie married William ("Sonny") Conklin, who Rose believes was related "somewhere in the woodpile" to his wife's (and Rose's) father, Jack.

According to this genealogy, Fred Conklin was a half-second cousin to his own mother and a half-first cousin twice

ABBREVIATED GENEALOGY: YOUMANS/CONKLIN

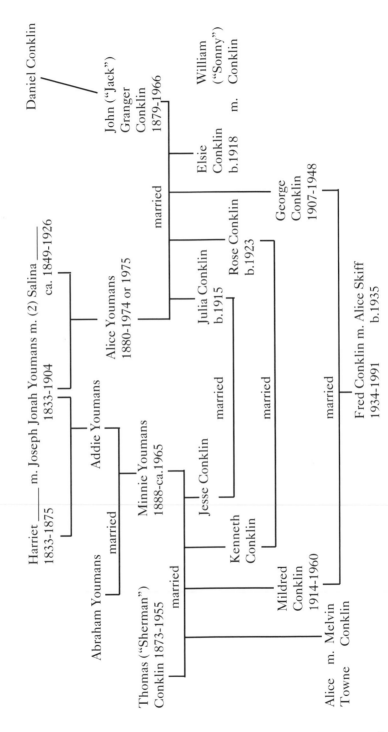

Daniel Conklin

Harriet _____ m. Joseph Jonah Youmans m. (2) Salina _____
1833-1875   1833-1904   ca. 1849-1926

Abraham Youmans   Addie Youmans

married

Alice Youmans
1880-1974 or 1975

married

John ("Jack")
Granger
Conklin
1879-1966

Elsie
Conklin
b.1918

William
("Sonny")
m.   Conklin

Minnie Youmans
1888-ca.1965

Jesse Conklin

married

Julia Conklin
b.1915

Rose Conklin
b.1923

George
Conklin
1907-1948

Thomas ("Sherman")
Conklin 1873-1955

married

Kenneth
Conklin

married

Mildred
Conklin
1914-1960

Fred Conklin m. Alice Skiff
1934-1991   b.1935

Alice   m.   Melvin
Towne   Conklin

married

9

removed to his father and was also a half-second cousin once removed to his own brothers and sisters. Rose Conklin Hogencamp, referring to her first marriage, told me, "I always remember knowing that my grandfather [Joseph Jonah Youmans] was my husband's great-grandfather."

The latter's gravestone (which misspells his name "Josept") gives the regiment numbers of his Civil War service and notes he died September 28, 1904, aged seventy-two. This would place his birth between September 1831 and September '32. But Rose told me she always understood that Joseph Jonah was born in 1833, "the year it rained the stars." When I asked what was meant by this phrase, Rose merely repeated it to me and implied it had never been fully explained to her. I have since learned that 1833 was the year of a spectacular display of the Leonid meteor shower, whose most extraordinary performances occur at intervals of approximately thirty-three years. Checking the muster of the 124th regiment we find that Joseph J. Youmans enlisted December 18, 1863, at age thirty. This would place his birth between December 1832 and December of '33, supporting the accuracy of his granddaughter's information. Rose's reference to the celestial event, quoted above, is a direct family tradition passed down orally for over a century and a half.

Fred's family drifted around a lot between Ulster County, Rockland County, and northern New Jersey. But every summer they'd return to the Shawangunk Mountains for berrypicking. The tarpaper shacks of the Conklin clan were on the first flat area above the Shingle Gully bridge, to the left of the road. Fred's uncles, aunts, and cousins on both sides camped here; both sets of grandparents summered here as well, until about the mid to late 1940s.

Fred and his siblings had far from an idyllic childhood and often suffered from being underfed and over-disciplined. "During the winter," Fred told me, "we lived up here on the old Goldie farm. Goin' up past the junkyard [off Cape Avenue, near the northwest boundary of Ellenville], there used to be a lot of hotels back in there years ago. This was a huge buildin', but we's only usin' two rooms outa the whole building. My father and mother slept in the same room they eat in, with a wood stove. We slept over 'cross a hallway, there was no heat, nothin' there, we had one blanket and an old pissed-up mattress what we laid on. Six boys, all on one mattress. And every one a' my brothers pissed in bed except me. I swear, we used to go in there some nights to lay down on that and there would be actually ice."

In 1949, as teenagers, Fred and his brother George (also known as Larry) camped at the Two-Mile Post from late summer or early fall all the way till after Christmas, having no place else to stay. The two boys managed to keep from freezing in the tarpaper shack by using a stove made from an old barrel.

Even summertime, when life was a bit easier than during the cold months, there were privations: Picking berries amongst the rocks and rattlesnakes and prickly scrub oak, "we had to go barefoot." And even the blueberries carpeting the mountainside were not quite free for the eating. "My father would say 'Come here young man,' he says, 'stick out your tongue.' So if he sees blue on your tongue, you got the hell knocked out. He says 'They belong in your bucket, not in your mouth,' that's what he used to tell us."

Fred told me some stories of encounters with the wild beasts of the mountain. The first occurred in the early 1940s.

> We went down to Ellenville to shop for groceries, my brother George, my brother Richard and myself. We were on our way back up the mountain, we had these sacks of groceries on our backs, they was feedbags. Nobody was thinkin' of nothing but just gettin' back up there. We was hurryin' 'cause it was gettin' dark, and our old man said "I want y's back here before it gets dark," you know. So anyway, this bobcat just jumped out right ahead of us. This was before you got up to the One-Mile Post, this happened. It no more than landed and all of a sudden the dog just went right after it. I

don't think it could have been more than fifteen feet from us.

Fred said the bobcat had jumped down off the bank from right to left and was probably as surprised as they were by the brief confrontation.

The following encounter occurred about the summer of 1943 or '44:

> *Me and my brother was in doin' the dishes, just talkin' and jokin' and laughin' and everything else. And we heard this noise outside the cabin. Then you could hear a snortin' sound. All of a sudden my brother he jumped, went in the far corner and he started yellin' "Lookit, lookit, there's a bear! There's a bear!" he kept sayin'. You know, I thought he was just jokin' with me. Sure enough, it was right there by the doorway. So he started screamin', I screamed; it bothered nobody—just took off and started down towards the Ellenville way.*

Fred's aunt Rose, who camped and picked berries here till about 1955, described a somewhat similar occurrence: "Joe Wilson was packin' to leave at the end of the summer and a bear come right down and stuck his snout in the camp door." Joe had seen the bear through the corner of his eye and thought it was the large dog named Laddie, belonging to Rose's sister. "I was talkin' to that bear and I thought it was the dog," he reportedly said.

Fred and his brothers had a few close calls with rattlesnakes, though no one ever got bit. He told me of one time in the early 1950s when a pair of rattlers had crawled up onto the frame of their cabin. This was the former store building, abandoned a year or two before, which the Conklins fixed up for their own use:

> *My brother Danny had went in first into the cabin, and he reached up like this, he was holdin' on one of the poles, and he felt somethin'. So he pulled down his*

hand real quick and one rattlesnake just come right off'n the pole. He fell out the back, on the outside of the cabin. But the other one didn't, he went out towards the back and dropped off and got into the foundation. We got one of the rattlesnakes.

Fred told me it was common for some of the folks who spent most of the summer at the Four- or Five-Mile Post to camp down at the Two-Mile for a couple of weeks early in the summer, until the berries ripened at the higher elevations. Similarly, some of the Two-Mile pickers would often relocate to the Four-Mile Post for the final weeks of the season, when the huckleberries were getting wormy down at the lower camp. It was thus that Fred, as a youngster, got to know an older generation of people who figured prominently in the huckleberry history of the Smiley Road: The Countryman family commonly picked at the Two-Mile Post early in the season, while in August, Fred's family often camped at the Four-Mile Post, in a cabin on the southeast side of the road, a short distance before Nina Addis's store. "We used to try to sneak one on Nina now and then," Fred told me. "Me, my half-brother Rich, and my brother Larry, we went out and we was gonna get ourselves some candy bars off'n Nina, right. So we took a lot of brush and we put it in the bottom of a quart basket. Then we put a little bit of berries over the top. But she went and told my father what we did. We got an awful tanning for it. We was gonna make a quick candy bar. That was just alongside the road, 'cause it was gettin' dark. I was up about two years ago talkin' to Nina and she remembered us doin' that."

When money was low, and oftentimes even when it wasn't low, many of the people would drink Sterno ("canned heat") fashioned into an alcoholic drink they called Pink Lady. Fred explained, "If ya was walkin' up that mountain, you bought a case of beer in Ellenville that's a hell of a long lug. But you can take a dozen cans of that, and in a sack, and carry it in one hand." Fred went on to describe for me the necessary procedure for making the concoction, which I am loath to repeat here lest it be misconstrued as an endorsement. "If you get the wax in, it could be a sudden death or total blindness, it tells you right on the can," he warned. "Lotta times Duckfoot would be the only one who had any money on him, and we used to say 'Please, c'mon make us up a bottle and we'll pay you when we pick blueberries.'"

"Duckfoot" was a man who camped here at the Two-Mile Post for a number of years, the nickname deriving from a physical handicap. I have not been able to learn his real name.

Fred Conklin and Hype Addis both remembered one or two families of African Americans who camped here during the 1940s. There was also a man of mixed blood, African and American Indian, who became friends with Hype. These

Hype Addis's store at the Two-Mile Post, 1949.

people apparently partied and socialized with the others at the Two-Mile Post without incurring racial unease.

"Kid" Dayton was remembered as a small, wiry man in his thirties, "a little bit on the slippery side." He was accused of stealing the pocketbook of one of the women at the Two-Mile Post. He was a fast berrypicker but a dirty one, with more than the usual allotment of twigs and leaves mixed in with his huckleberries. Rose Conklin Hogencamp told me, "He'd go out with a berrybox on his back and pickin' basket tied on top of the box and two metal pails, and he'd be back in the camp before the others were ready to start pickin'." Fred Conklin said he once caught Dayton with a bucket on the ground, just "thrashin' the bushes" with his hand. "I don't know how he ever got Hype to buy his berries, they were so dirty," Fred told me.

The Williams family, which included two boys and their mother and stepfather, picked berries at the Two-Mile Post intermittently during the 1940s but did not enjoy a salutary reputation. "I didn't like them in no shape or manner," Rose Hogencamp told me. "They stole my hound dog and took it to Sam's Point. But I got him back." This happened about 1945 or '46, according to Fred.[1]

Hype Addis, who took over the former Ben Conklin store here at the Two-Mile Post, has amended his former recollections and concluded that he had his store during 1949 and 1950, not '48 and '49 as he'd previously recalled. He measured berries here for Grover Perkins both years. Hype

---

[1] In *Tales from the Shawangunk Mountains* (pp.94-97), I wrote of Roy "Dime" Towne (born 1882) being an early and longtime berrypicker at the Two-Mile Post until his death about 1950; but doubt is raised by Fred Conklin, who remembered Dime Towne being here for only one year (during the forties), and by information to the effect that Dime had spent many years incarcerated. Dime's brother George and the latter's son John (born 1925) camped here for six or seven years about the thirties and early forties according to John, but the latter could not recall if other members of the family had been here. Dime Towne's daughter Alice married Melvin Conklin, a brother of Fred's mother, Mildred; I also wrote of Mel and Alice's connection with the Two-Mile Post, but both Fred and his aunt Rose, as well as another informant, tell me that Mel and Alice and their family were not present at the Two-Mile Post nearly as much as I'd been led to believe.

bought berries in 1950 on Rock Haven Road and late-season berries that same summer at the Five-Mile Post, but he did not become a berry buyer in his own right at the Two- and Four-Mile posts until 1951, after Grover had retired from the business. Hype's store was located on a little semicircular shelf atop a retaining wall, on the left-hand side of the road, above the Conklin shanties. Immediately below the store, on the opposite side of the road, were the water barrels, under a big pine tree that stands there yet. Hype told me that one time the Williams family got Kid Dayton drunk and talked him into breaking the lock on his store. The Williamses allegedly cleaned out the contents of the store, "fifty or sixty dollars worth of food and booze." The next summer, Dayton paid Hype back every cent of the money, though he had not benefited from the spoils. The Williams family moved to Sam's Point.

Above the site of the store is a large flat area on the same side of the road, where many cabins stood. There were cabins across the road on the right-hand side as well. Some of the people who camped here were Ben and Hilda Slover; Grover and Agnes Quick, with their sons Virgil and Sonny and daughter Alice; also Jesse and Lil Starr, with four or five children. The Slovers and Quicks spent time at the Four-Mile Post as well as the Two-Mile, the Quicks' last year on the mountain being about 1942. About 1942/43 the Starr family spent much of an entire winter in a shanty here at the Two-Mile Post, the children walking all the way down and back up the mountain on the occasions when they attended school. This arrangement was terminated by the police, and the children were eventually put in foster homes, out of concern for their welfare.

Fred Conklin's father died in 1948; his mother camped at the Two-Mile Post with the family till about the early fifties. In 1955 Fred married Alice Skiff, who'd camped and picked berries at the Four- and Five-Mile posts with her mother, May, and brothers Ed, Tom, and Frank. They had been berrypickers since sometime in the 1940s, when they began sharing a cabin with Herman Countryman. Herman had been friendly with the Skiff family for some years prior to this, and the younger Skiff children, including Alice, had grown up thinking of Herman almost as a father. In the summer of 1955, shortly after the great August flood, May Skiff broke her ankle while walking up the Smiley Road toward the Two-Mile Post. The road was virtually impassable, and Fred's car had been destroyed by the deluge; so May, a heavy woman, was placed on a bedspring and carried down the mountain by Fred and some others. Herman was up at the Four-Mile Post at the time. That was the last summer the Skiff family camped on the Smiley Road, but Fred and Alice continued their summer berrypicking here for nearly another decade. Soon they were raising a family of their own, and another generation of Conklins were spending their childhood summers here at the Two-Mile Post.

After Nina Addis departed from the Four-Mile Post with the last of her berrypicking companions, the Two-Mile Post, with its greater accessibility and proximity to the valley, retained the only vestige of commercial berrypicking on the Smiley Road. During the final years, when there was no longer a usable cabin here, the following continued to join the Conklins picking huckleberries: Art and Dorothy Thompson; Fred's brother George; Oscar Countryman, who had stayed at the Four-Mile till Nina's last year; and Fred's aunt Elsie Conklin. In addition, the following were occasional weekend campers here: Sam ("Chuck") Hogencamp, whose father, Charles, was the second husband of Fred's aunt Rose (Chuck later married Sandy Conklin, who is Rose's daughter from her first marriage); Elsie Conklin's husband, William ("Sonny") Conklin; one Frank Annacone; and Roy Hemion and his wife, Pat (Roy is Dorothy Thompson's son). Roy often entertained the group with music. He knew an endless number of songs, according to Fred, and played guitar, mouth organ, and Jew's harp. Fred himself played mouth organ around the evening campfire.

These people slept outside on mattresses atop old bedsprings, with Fred and Alice's children spending the night in the back of their pickup truck. A plastic tarp provided protection from brief showers, but when inclement weather persisted, the people simply left the mountain until conditions improved. Fred's maternal aunt Doris Stewart and perhaps a few others were occasional day-pickers at the camp. Herman and Art Countryman occasionally camped for a few nights during these summers.

Most of these people were present on and off through the summer of 1961 or '62. During the very last couple of years, through about the summer of '64, Fred and Alice and their children and Oscar Countryman were all who remained. Oscar was still together with his common-law wife, Evelyn, but they were having problems, so she did not join him on the mountain. Oscar, whose legs were getting wobbly by now, would often stay in camp and watch the children while Fred and Alice went out to pick berries. Fred remembered his last summer up here was the driest in memory: He had to hike to a spring fifteen minutes through the woods, directly up the mountain slope, to fetch water.

In the early 1950s, the Conklins generally sold their huckleberries to Hype Addis. After the flood, Fred began marketing berries to a wholesaler in Middletown, unless he was low on gas or had accumulated only a few crates of fruit, when he'd sell them locally to bakeries. From the late fifties through his final year at the Two-Mile Post, he usually brought the berries down to New Jersey. On these occasions (usually twice a week), the whole family, with Oscar, would pack up and ride down together. This is apparently why I missed seeing them when I passed by this way on foot, once or twice during the summer of 1962, on my first hikes up the Smiley Road from Ellenville.

After 1964 the Conklins no longer earned a significant part of their income picking berries. But until about the early seventies, they'd still make a couple of berrypicking trips to the Two-Mile Post each summer: They'd spend a few nights under the stars, before returning to the valley to sell their huckleberries, mostly to Albert's Bakery in Ellenville.

I last saw Fred in October of 1991; eight months had passed since my previous visit, and I sang him a few songs I'd written since then about the huckleberry pickers. I was delighted by his favorable response to the tunes. Less than two weeks later, Fred Conklin was dead.

It was perhaps his great strength and his failing as well, that Fred seemed never to transcend his roots, that he appeared at times to be consumed by the forces that had molded his youth. If these traits left him with some bitterness and also with some handicaps (he was virtually unable to read and write, though by no means deficient in native intelligence), they also marked him as a person of uncommon genuineness and openness, a man who earned the fierce loyalties of the extended family of children and grandchildren whose cottages formed a cluster with his own, close by the base of the mountain's northwest slope. Fred possessed a rare authenticity of character, and I felt fortunate to count him as a friend.

Despite many ill memories of a less-than-lovely childhood, there was a part of his past that haunted Fred Conklin with an attraction that was more than he himself could explain.

> *From a baby I was carried into the mountains. It was just a thing, that every year you looked forward to get there, you couldn't wait. You just couldn't wait to get up there. It's like, it's in your soul, you can't get out of it. If you was livin' it; if you could go there and live it like I lived it. . . and my brothers, . . . it was a great thing to go to each year. There's something that draws you back there every year. It was just like some kind of a power, pulling. There's something inside of me I can't bring out. I just loved it. It was just something like holding you there.*

Fred lies buried on a hillside at Fantinekill. When the trees are bare, there's a view from his gravesite directly across the narrow valley to where the Shingle Gully takes its precipitous course down the mountainside. I should think that his home of seventeen years, near the bottom of this stream, and the huckleberry camp where he spent his youth, are thus close enough to his final resting place to allow of peaceful slumbers for a man so deeply rooted in his past, or of the occasional nocturnal ramble, should his spirit be so inclined.

Chapter 2

Around the Bowl
of the Witch's Hole

A few minutes past the Two-Mile Post, we come upon the wreck of an old truck lying overturned in the bushes to the left of the road. The truck was headed up the mountain when it apparently experienced some kind of mechanical or structural failure. It stood abandoned in the middle of the road for some days before being winched out of the way to its ultimate demise by some hunters whose egress by jeep was being blocked by the abandoned vehicle. It was reportedly owned by two brothers who were using it to carry a stove up to their hunting cabin near the Four-Mile Post.

Five minutes later we enter a narrow strip of land that is part of the New York State Forest Preserve. The "forever wild" status of this holding posed a potential problem for the Smiley family at the time they were laying out the route of their road. An inquiry by Edward A. Smiley early in 1900 prompted a reply from William F. Fox, Superintendent of State Forests, informing Mr. Smiley that "a forestry clause in the new constitution. . . forbids the use of any State land by a private interest."

"At the same time," Supt. Fox hastened to add, "the Commissioners would like to assist you in every possible way . . . ." Apparently the right-of-way across state land would be perfectly legal, "provided it was asked for by the town, and laid out across the lot as a town road, . . . in which case I think there would be no trouble in obtaining the desired permit to cross the land irrespective of the fact that the remainder of the road might be a private road." In a follow-up letter dated May 7, 1900, Supt. Fox wrote that "the Commissioners express themselves as doubtful whether they could give written permission. They decided, however, that, as the road had been laid out officially by the highway commissioner, they would interpose no objections to your driving across the State land . . . and that you are at liberty to construct the road accordingly."

So as I understand it, the venerable commissioners could not give written permission, but on the other hand felt it perfectly proper to convey to Mr. Smiley, through the Superintendent's letter, that "you are at liberty to construct the road"—a maneuver whose legal and semantic contortions bear a striking resemblance to the double switchbacks in the road itself near its Ellenville end. As we proceed up the mountain, the thought occurs that perhaps this segment of the Smiley Road, "laid out as a town road," yet falls under the jurisdiction of the highway department of the Town of Wawarsing; I shall consider the efficacy of complaining forthwith to the highway superintendent regarding the roadbed's deplorable condition!

The rightward curve of the road becomes more pronounced as we continue our steady climb, till the reason for the diversion becomes evident when a panorama opens up across the great expanse of Louis Ravine or the Witch's Hole. It is well worth a rest stop at this vantage point, for the view across to the magnificent white cliffs of Napanoch Point and vicinity is easily the finest to be enjoyed along the entire length of the Smiley Road without leaving the roadbed itself.

Several minutes after departing this overlook, we cross a small brook, the first of the ravine's main tributaries. About seven or eight minutes farther, a small depression on the left side of the road reveals, upon close inspection, an opening in the ground just large enough for a person of narrow frame and curious bent to lower himself into. A friend of mine who fits that description managed to fit himself down into that hole and found himself in a tiny room, with sufficient clearance to kneel and peer over the edge of a vertical shaft that descends about another ten feet. With flashlight in hand, he was able to discern what appeared to be a widening at the bottom of the shaft, with possibly another chamber.

We discovered this cave on a frigid February day that followed upon weeks of relatively mild weather. A visible mist of condensed water vapor was rising from the opening, coating the surrounding bushes with frost. My companion found some large spider webs inside with large spiders, but no hibernating rattlesnakes; nevertheless, the wisdom of climbing into a hole with such restricted visibility and freedom of movement would be questionable during the warmer months, when such serpents as might be encountered would be wide awake.

A couple of minutes farther along the road, we arrive at the site of the Three-Mile Post, where a rocky path along a small, overgrown, and often dry streambed climbs the slope on our right to High Point, a mile distant. This path was used as a firebreak to contain blazes that occurred on the mountain in 1947 and 1953. The fires burned the area west of the trail, and the action of either fire or fire fighters destroyed the trees on that side. As we stand at the trail junction, looking toward High Point, the woods to our right consist of relatively young growth, mostly birches, whereas east of the trail we can see a mixed forest including some sizeable pines and chestnut oaks.

Ben Conklin had a store and cabin on the right-hand side of the Smiley Road, a little past this trail junction. The living quarters came first, with a door on the northwest side, opening toward the footpath. The store shared one wall with the cabin and had its door on the southeast side. Ben does not appear to be related to Fred Conklin or to Fred's ancestors on either side; but through Ben's mother, Julia Rose Conklin, Ben was a first cousin to Bill Countryman and to Nina Addis's mother, Elizabeth. Julia and a few of Ben's children and grandchildren camped here during most of the 1930s. When the Three-Mile Post was disbanded late in that decade, many of its inhabitants went down the road to the Two-Mile Post. Ben Conklin moved

Ben Conklin and his third wife, in a photograph taken 1972.

his store there, before moving on to Sam's Point. Some of his family told me Ben was at Sam's Point from 1944 on, while Hype Addis and Fred Conklin are equally certain Ben had a store at the Two-Mile Post through the summer of '48. Perhaps he divided his time between the two locations during these years. Ben was skilled at weaving baskets from saplings cut in the mountains, and in later years he made and sold some of these to supplement his income.

Another couple of minutes up the road, on our right, about where the road emerges from the Forest Preserve, there's a never-failing spring of water that goes by the name of Rickety Spring. A modern plastic pipe, ugly but functional, has been fitted onto what remains of the rusting iron pipe of yore. Before continuing eastward, we'll stop and quench our thirst in a toast to the many hundreds of berrypickers who drank from this same spring in a bygone era.

Rose Conklin Hogencamp, born July 1923, camped with her family at the Three-Mile Post from the summer of 1931 until they were forced to relocate at the Two-Mile Post later in the decade. Their first year they stayed in a tent on the right-hand side of the road, about halfway between Ben's store and Rickety Spring. Thereafter they lived in a tarpaper shack a little beyond the spring and across the road, on the left-hand side. Rose confirms what others have said, that the Three-Mile Post was about the largest of the Smiley Road huckleberry communities. "That was a city up there," she told me. Besides Ben Conklin's store there was a smaller store, a few minutes' walk farther up the road from Rose's cabin, on the same side as the latter. This was owned by Ed Davis, who had two boys, Carl and Walter. Hype Addis remembers Davis would make trips once or twice a week up the mountain to the Four- and Five-Mile posts in a great big touring car, "a Huffmobile, something like that," with a large cooler strapped on the back; he'd sell ice cream sandwiches and pops, and he'd buy some berries directly from the pickers, marketing the berries in Kingston. Rose recalls Ed selling fresh milk and buttermilk to the campers out of forty-quart cans. Sometimes the layer of cream on top of the milk would be well on its way to becoming butter by the time it reached the Three- or Four-Mile Post.

Rose and her sister Julia told me the story of a man at the Three-Mile Post, Lester Patterson, who had two young boys about Rose's age. The boys were named Alvin and Norman. Their father was very hard with them and beat them when they didn't pick enough huckleberries. He was also a fierce drinker who generally drank up the proceeds of his sons' labors. An early riser, he used to rouse the whole camp by bellowing, "Whoopie! Wake up, snakes, and get yer likker!"

Rose recalls only a few names of other campers here during the early and mid thirties: Pete Quick and his wife, Carrie (who later moved to the Four-Mile Post), and Joe and Bess Porter. Pete was the father of Grover Quick, whom I've mentioned in connection with the Two-Mile Post, and was a brother to Nina Addis's father, Albert. Pete'd "rather fight than eat," according to his grand-nephew Hype Addis. Apparently old Pete'd also rather *drink* than eat, though I never learned whether he preferred drinking to fighting. One evening when Pete was already getting on in years and living in a little cabin on North Mountain Road, west of Benton's Corners, Winslow Van Leuven found him lying in the middle of Bruynswick Road, drunk, and barely stopped the car in time to avoid running him over. Pete died in July 1938 while camping at the Four-Mile Post.

Hype Addis was raised at the Four-Mile Post but has some early recollections of the Three-Mile, which he'd pass whenever ascending or descending the mountain in the family automobile. Most of the cabins were on the same side of the road as Ben's store, he remembers. At Rickety Spring there were three water barrels. About thirty or forty feet before the spring, on the left-hand side as you ascend the road, one berrypicker had built his sleeping quarters elevated a few feet above the ground, in a clump of trees. Below was a lean-to where he kept his belongings.

> *This was back in the thirties, it was a large campground, just on the other side of the waterin' barrel there was a man that had his bed built in the trees. He had a roof overhead, he had a regular little treehouse just big enough for a bed, that's all. The whole thing was built of saplings like a little bamboo hut with a roof onto it. It was just big enough for him to crawl into. And that's where he slept nights; as a kid I always figured it was 'cause he was afraid of animals: snakes, animals, everything. 'Cause back in those days a bobcat used to run around once in a while, he used to screech a little bit once in a while. I was only a little kid, we just saw it passin' through. But I can remember that now, I can picture that in my mind.*

A few minutes past Rickety Spring, the remains of a tailfinned 1957 Chevy station wagon grace the underbrush on the left side of the road. The car is upright and, like the old truck a mile farther back, is facing uphill. I have been unable to learn anything concerning its demise, but I seem to remember it already here when I first passed this way in the summer of 1962. That would make it a relatively new car when its driver chose to navigate the post-flood Smiley Road, and its fate should perhaps not have been unanticipated. During the mid 1960s, I myself made a brief attempt with my similarly low-slung '56 Olds; by the time I'd reached that first killer curve perhaps a hundred yards up from the flats in Ellenville, the car had suffered enough loud, grinding thumps on its undercarriage to make me shift into reverse, happy to make good my escape.

Eight or ten minutes past Rickety Spring we arrive at Beaver Creek, the main watercourse of Louis Ravine. This brook is rarely dry but now must be forded without benefit of a bridge, hardly a problem, however, since the streambed lies scarcely lower than the road on either side. The bridge was reportedly washed away in the '55 flood but was apparently recovered or replaced, for I remember it from my early walks along the road. The tents and cabins of berrypickers formerly dotted the road from the Three-Mile Post as far as this point. At the behest of the Napanoch prison authorities, the pickers were chased off the Beaver Creek (which runs directly down to the prison reservoir, near the bottom of the ravine) about the beginning of the 1930s, several years before the shacks were destroyed at the Three-Mile Post proper. But some of the people kept returning, with tents, on and off until about the early forties, I am told. Day pickers still visited their old camping grounds in the area till about the end of that decade. The Beaver Creek vicinity was always populated predominantly by Germans. After coming over from Sam's Point and prior to settling up at the Four-Mile Post, the man known to all as Blacky camped here on the right-hand side of the road, just before the creek crossing.

A few minutes past the creek, a good jeep trail comes down off the slope from the right. This leads southward and southwestward through beaver-built wetlands to join the Fire Tower Road at the base of High Point. It was built about 1967 by the company that brought seismographs to test for natural gas caverns deep below the mountain.

The Smiley Road soon begins a steady ascent, leaving behind the deep, moist woods that characterize the road's passage through the upper reaches of Louis Ravine. Finally it breaks through the cliff line and onto level bedrock in a sweeping rightward curve that marks its moment of transformation: Between here and the Stony Kill the road will traverse a section of the great Shawangunk Mountain pine barrens. If one were to visualize the Smiley Road in a generic sense, this would be the portion most likely to come to mind. Many a time I have bushwhacked through this region, following an azimuth through thick vegetation so as to pick up the road near some predetermined location. The pine barrens, always formidable, are beginning to seem endless, when suddenly and always without the slightest premonition, I've found myself upon this rock-studded, sun- and shade-speckled pathway, this sweet haven for the bush-weary tramper. A familiar friend in the thick of the wilderness, it is long-sought, but somehow no less unexpected when finally it arrives.

Two minutes above the great curve in the road, a narrow but well-trodden footpath leads off to the left. We will follow this for several minutes, past some minor lookouts, to Napanoch Point, one of the major scenic overlooks of the Shawangunk ridge. From here there is a dramatic, plunging view down through the Witch's Hole, with its cliff-lined tributaries. To our left we follow with our eyes the great horseshoe bend of the escarpment, to High Point, the latter peering out over the nearly level, forested swamps of the ravine's uppermost regions, from a vantage point some three hundred feet above us. To our right, below the mountain, the green-domed edifice of the old Napanoch prison is partially visible to the side of one of the false summits that rise in boldly curving silhouette against the valley floor. One-third mile northward along the escarpment from where we stand is the Hanging Rock. The walk will reward us with even more breathtaking views of this spectacular ravine.

Returning to the Smiley Road we continue our trek eastward, at a fairly level grade. After about thirty yards we come upon an inscription visible in the bedrock to our right; this will be explained later, in context. A minute farther, on our left, a jeep trail begins its descent of three miles through the pine barrens and the gully of Mine Hole Brook, to Foordmoor Road, at the base of the mountain. This jeep trail was constructed about 1983 or '84 by a group of hunters who had built a cabin several years earlier near the upper section of the trail. The trail approximately followed an old right-of-way that presumably was used for taking berries, timber, or hoop saplings down from the mountain. A 1909 deed from Henry and Mary Green conveys to Dr. Andrew Green Foord a nine hundred-acre parcel of land on the mountain, in and above the aforementioned gully,

> *excepting and reserving. . . a road or way over the premises. . . leading from the old turnpike road which leads from New Paltz to Wawarsing [present-day Foordmoor Road] and which road so reserved is to extend from said turnpike to the lot known as the Whitaker lot [i.e., through the extent of the lands hereby conveyed] by way of the gum swamp as said road is now laid out and used.*

Three minutes farther, just after a little rise and a right-hand curve in the Smiley Road, a pathway leads on the right across open rocks about a hundred yards to the ruins of another hunters' cabin, referred to previously: This was reportedly built about the early 1970s by those who owned the truck that lies abandoned above the Two-Mile Post.

The berrypickers' shanties of the Four-Mile Post began to dot the roadside from about this point eastward. About thirty

Fred Conklin (center), family members, and the author (right) stop for refreshment during a hike along the Smiley Road, September 1989.

yards farther along, a few rocks are visible among the bushes on our right, perhaps twenty-five yards from the road's edge. Here was the shack of Grover and Agnes Quick, who divided their time between the Two- and Four-Mile posts, and in this shack Grover's father, Pete, passed away. Another thirty-five or forty yards, we come to a partially moss-covered rock outcrop on the right, elevated several feet above the roadbed. Here, about twenty feet from the road, was the cabin of Elliott Addis (no known relation to Hype Addis) and his common-law partner, Flo Floshay, who camped here until about the early or mid 1940s. About thirty-five yards farther along the road, on our right, was the cabin where Fred Conklin and his folks stayed during the latter part of each summer. There were a few other cabins here as well.

The road dips a little, then rises slightly, up onto an outcropping. On our right, about forty yards from the edge of the road, was a good cabin with wooden siding and a board floor. A number of people stayed here over the years, including Blacky, before the latter got his own cabin, farther east on the site of the Van Leuven store. Hype recalls a man known as "Mike the Polack" who used this wooden cabin for a time. "He had a pair of store teeth that he ordered through the catalog for five dollars," Hype said. "Every time he talked the top teeth'd go dropping down, he had to push 'em back up. He said it was the best teeth that ever fitted him.

"Back in those days," Hype continued, "I was about ten or twelve years old, in the late 1930s, and I had pinworms, and he said one of the best things to cure pinworms was kerosene, so my mother gave me a tablespoon of kerosene. I burped kerosene bubbles for two days. But I still had the pinworms."

Another twenty-five or thirty yards along our way, a footpath crosses the Smiley Road at the heart of the Four-Mile Post. On our right, the path leads up across the Badlands toward High Point, some two miles distant, and on the other side it descends through equally rough terrain to Decker's Pond, Rock Haven Road, and Kerhonkson. At the trail junction on the Smiley Road, a large cross or compass painted on the bedrock directs the traveler to High Point, Kerhonkson, Ellenville, and "OVASTING LAKE."

On the right-hand side of the road, about forty feet along the footpath south of this compass, was the cabin of a man from Virginia named John. "'Saint John' we used to call him," Hype told me. "He liked to do a little preaching. He'd talk a little sermon on Sunday and then naturally he'd go out and get a little drunk himself. He was there till the late forties." After Saint John's departure the cabin was taken over by Ben and Hilda Slover.

On the left side of the Smiley Road, directly across from the compass, was the long, narrow cabin of Wilson and Mary (Van Wagner) Quick. This was located about fifty feet from the edge of the road; in between is a small area of rock outcrop.

At the Quicks' Cabin, Four-Mile Post, August 1943. Left to right: (standing) Lawrence Addis, his daughter June, Elliot Addis and a little girl named Mary-Lou, Frank Quick, Mr. Ross; (seated) Mary Quick, Flo Floshay.

Mary had a little vegetable garden just to the right of this outcrop. Her son Frank Quick planted a couple of peach trees there as well. These are now gone, but an apple tree planted in later years, possibly by Blacky, stands there yet. The cabin is believed to have stood until the late summer or early autumn of 1958. The family was originally from Napanoch, then moved about 1936 to Oakville, Connecticut, near Waterbury. After that, Wilson came up only on weekends, but Mary and Frank stayed and picked berries all summer. Frank was born in 1928 and spent his last summer at the Four-Mile Post about 1948. His mother stayed on through the summer of '49 or '50. The family had camped there for over thirty years all told, and prior to that had made day trips to pick berries up on the Jacob's Ladder.

During one August about a year before he left the mountain, Frank and a family by the name of Smith, from

Florida, sold their berries and those of one other family directly to bakeries and markets in the mid-Hudson region, making about three trips per week; this was because they were unhappy with the prices being paid by Grover Perkins, the outside buyer for whom Nina measured. Frank used to catch rattlesnakes live, though his original intention of selling them to medical laboratories never panned out. Years earlier, at the age of about ten, while picking berries with his family between the Four-Mile Post and High Point, the party ran into a rattlesnake den and killed three large ones including a rattler reputedly measuring 6'1" in length.

The footpath that descends the mountain from the Smiley Road at the site of Mary Quick's cabin merges, after a few minutes, with an alternate, more easterly branch of the same trail, which leaves the Smiley Road about fifty yards farther along from here. The path (except for the west branch) was marked with yellow paint in 1960 along an old silver-painted and cairn-marked trail. Blue paint was added in 1975, following the yellow path down toward the northeast and eventually branching off to the left to follow a streambed down to Foordmoor Road near the Ukrainian resort.

There is another footpath that comes up from the valley and terminates near here. In order to become familiar with the several junctions and side branches, we'll walk a ways down the overgrown trail on our left, as if heading for Decker's and Kerhonkson on this westerly branch: We cross a small streambed known to the pickers as Mossy Brook and ascend to some outcrops on the other side of the thicket, where a row of cairns immediately leads off to our right, paralleling the swale and then bearing left to join the east branch of the yellow-marked trail. If we continue on our original route without taking this short connecting link, we very soon come to another junction, at about the point where the Rondout Reservoir becomes visible some miles off in the distance. The trail descending at an angle slightly to our left here will be described presently.

Continuing straight ahead on the main trail will soon merge us with the east branch at a point a couple of minutes farther along, thus forming a loop with the connecting link previously referred to. This yellow trail was in later years called by some of the berrypickers the Tombstone Path, so named for a flat rock, gravestone-shaped but with a concave top edge, propped up on end about seven minutes down along the path from the road. This was known as "Fred Crose's Resting Rock," after the man who set it in place and used to sit on it for a final rest stop, on his way back up to the Four-Mile Post with his day's harvest of huckleberries. Fred's cabin was on the north side of the Smiley Road, about thirty feet from the road, directly across from the board cabin used by Blacky, Mike the Polack, and others. Fred was a nephew of Caleb Crose, who married Mary Caston, about whom more will be said in due course. According to Hype Addis, Fred was an intelligent, likeable fellow. He was a "periodic drunkard," who, after some time spent on the wagon, would typically go off on a phenomenal drinking binge including Sterno and anything else that might be available. He died about 1946 or '47 and on his rock was inscribed a message in black paint or tar, in memoriam, by the berrypicker known as Saint John. This inscription has been obliterated by time and by the scrawlings of a latter-day painter.

It is a pleasant walk down the Tombstone Path toward Rock Haven Road, with many open areas of rock outcrop. The path crosses a stream (Polack Brook or the Little Stony Kill) at a delightful place filled with the music of flowing water. There are fine vistas down the streambed to the blue domes of the Catskill Mountains. It is not difficult for one's imagination to picture Nina Addis and her ragtag companions, loaded down with huckleberries, stopping here for a rest some summer afternoon nearly forty years ago, on their way down the mountain to sell their berries to Nina's son Hype, who'd meet them at George Decker's place.

Just below the crossing place, on the southeast side of the brook, is an elevated outcrop known as Pulpit Rock. Here the group of berrypickers would abandon the old footpath in favor of a nearly parallel fire access trail lying a couple of hundred yards to the east. This fire trail was the route used by Hype

At Ross's Cabin (Near Saint John's Camp), Four-Mile Post, 1944.
Left to right: (standing) Mary Quick, Fred Crose, Nina Addis;
(seated) Lawrence Addis, Mr. Ross.

Addis to haul canned goods and other supplies up to Nina's
store with his farm tractor, at the beginning of each season
during Nina's last few years at the Four-Mile Post.
Unfortunately, the historic link between the Smiley and Rock
Haven roads is no longer usable as a public through-route, due
to the policy of those who succeeded George Decker as
proprietors. But the hiker may descend as far as Pulpit Rock
and return to the Smiley Road via the fire trail, without
infringing on private land.

If we bear left at the second trail junction across the swale
from the Four-Mile Post, instead of following the Tombstone
Path, we will find ourselves descending the uppermost portion
of a different footpath: one leading all the way down the
mountainside to Port Ben (East Wawarsing), a small settlement
on the Berme Road. This route's lower portion, which follows a
brook in a gully of considerable depth, was used by generations

of huckleberry pickers, who climbed up from their homes in the valley to pick for the day, returning the same evening. Where the path ascends steeply through a notch in the cliff line, three-quarters of a mile north-northeast of Napanoch Point, is the Jacob's Ladder, named for the ladder from earth to heaven that Jacob saw in a dream.

Near the bottom of Jacob's Ladder is a spring of drinking water that some referred to as a "tide spring." On the way up in the morning, the pickers would fill their jugs with the cold, clear water; valley-bound late in the afternoon, they would often find the spring dry. Many of the pickers supposed the spring to be influenced by sea tides, though mid-day evaporation from the watershed above the spring is a more credible explanation. The path from the top of the Ladder down the mountain has been marked in relatively recent years with metal tags and red paint, to where the path encounters a jeep trail coming up through the gully from Berme Road. This land is privately owned and posted.

From the top of Jacob's Ladder the route climbs southward one-quarter of a mile to a peculiar, isolated ledge of bedrock that forms a miniature summit, with a view all around. This spot has long been known as Panther Rock because a panther (mountain lion) was said to have been sighted here years ago. The monolith bears the initials WBM and the date 1941, originally done in a dark blue-green, now legible only because the paint, which has disappeared, left its white "shadow" on the rock where lichen has not yet grown in. This rock was shown to me in the late summer of 1989 by Don Munro of Saugerties, who never picked huckleberries much, but who'd been hunting in this part of the mountain for some forty years. He and several companions constructed the jeep trail referred to earlier that connects the Smiley Road near Napanoch Point with Foordmoor Road, via Mine Hole Gully. The path up from Jacob's Ladder crosses this jeep trail a short distance before Panther Rock.

Following old cairns and relying oftentimes on Don's memory, we were able to trace the portion of the old path from

Panther Rock on up to the Four-Mile Post. The route follows for the most part across bare rocks overlooking the swale that has its origin at the Four-Mile Post and empties down over the cliff line between the Jacob's Ladder and the Hanging Rock. In three places above the initialed rock, the blue-green paint of nearly fifty years earlier, which followed the older, cairn-marked trail, was still visible to confirm the route. Near its upper end the swale branches, and we had to drop off the rocks and bushwhack through thick woods to cross the left branch. Here my guide's memory was indispensable as he led the way down into the mossy streambed at a spot known as the "knee-breaker," where a flat rock placed between small ledges serves as a stepping-stone to climb back up out of the hollow.

From the Four-Mile Post to Panther Rock, a friend and I have since restored the path with the placement of additional cairns. We did the same between Panther Rock and Jacob's Ladder, though here we were forced to rely a good deal on the compass, because of the scarcity of old cairns and difficulty in determining the precise original route.

Frank Quick told me of a time, one September when he was twelve years old, when he hiked with his parents down along this path from the Four-Mile Post to the Gum Swamp (black gum or pepperidge trees), just below the Jacob's Ladder, to harvest wild honey. They went after dark and cut down a honey tree that they'd located previously during daylight hours. They were rewarded with a harvest of about sixty pounds, which they carried all the way back to the Four-Mile Post in the dark. About a year later they found another tree in the same swamp and made a similar nighttime excursion, but got a more modest ten or fifteen pounds of honey for their labors. The next day they made the mistake of burning the empty comb in the cabin's stove: "All the bees in the whole mountain must've smelled it, and came and chased us right outa the cabin," Frank remembers.

The possibility exists that the origins of this Jacob's Ladder path may go back much farther into the past than the berrypickers themselves ever suspected. A published account written in 1820 by Charles G. De Witt, describing an Indian attack on a dwelling in the town of Shawangunk some forty years earlier, refers to an "Indian footpath, leading directly across the mountain," nine miles from the foot of the mountain in Shawangunk "to the first habitation on the other side. . . ." Rev. Charles Scott, writing in the 1861 *Collections of the Ulster Historical Society*, states the following, after referring to an Indian village on the bank of the Shawangunk Kill: "From this village a pathway, yet preserved, led across the mountains to Wawarsink. . . . This was the Wawarsink trail, so well known to all the early inhabitants of Shawangunk and Rochester." In the same volume he elsewhere observes that the trail passed "by Awosting Lake—the Long Pond. . . ."

Other early writers have given somewhat conflicting accounts. By the nineteenth century there may have been a number of modern branches off of the original Indian trail, and it is doubtful any of these writers could speak with certainty. And yet I am convinced that the Jacob's Ladder path is a prime contender for the original route of this old Wawarsing Trail.

It is widely accepted, on the basis of both oral tradition and historical research, that the confluence of the Vernooy Kill and Rondout Creek, one-third mile northeast of the bridge at Port Ben, is the likely site of the main settlement of the Esopus Indians. This is believed to be the location of the fortified village destroyed by Dutch soldiers in July of 1663. The Indians, not having the facilities to map or survey the top of the mountain with precision, would likely have followed natural routes of travel where possible, straying somewhat from the shortest route as easily determined today by a glance at the modern topographical map. The gully and stream leading up the mountain from a point just southwest of Port Ben would have provided just such an easily identifiable natural pathway. The passage thence through the Jacob's Ladder and perhaps up as far as the Four-Mile Post could well be the same route followed for centuries by the aboriginal inhabitants and, later, by early settlers of the Rondout Valley. The possibility thus exists that huckleberry pickers of the nineteenth and twentieth centuries were simply following a trail that had been in continual use since prehistoric times.

From Panther Rock another line of cairns and one barely discernible spot of the old blue-green paint mark a trail leading northeastward about one-half of a mile to a small run of water, along the far side of which stand a number of large, brownish-gray rocks of exotic origin, deposited by the glacier during its southward journey eons ago. The cairns abruptly end here before recontinuing intermittently, through areas now overgrown, to the vicinity of a certain spring of water known to all the huckleberry pickers as Hank Green's Spring. Hype Addis and I tried unsuccessfully to rediscover this spring before Hype was led to the spot by Irvin Decker and Frances (Decker) Barringer, both of Kerhonkson.

The spring is most easily found by first locating a large cairn that stands atop a twenty-foot ledge of bedrock at about the 1540-foot contour of the USGS topographical map, eleven hundred yards due west of the center of Decker's Pond. From Pulpit Rock, previously described, descend at an angle along the easiest route to Polack Brook, then continue downstream about two and a half minutes to where a line of cairns crosses. Walk west-northwest, following the cairns, some of which are original and some recently rebuilt.

Directly along the path is an odd pattern of looped and intersecting furrows in the surface of the bedrock, the fossilized tracks of large worms slithering through the still-soft Shawangunk sediments of over four hundred million years ago. The path branches after five minutes or so: The original route bears right and approaches the spring from below, through an area now badly overgrown; the easier approach is to bear left and climb to the top of the twenty-foot ledge, then walk north and northwestward along the edge for a minute or two, until a large oak tree is spotted below and to the northwest, through a break in the vegetation. Descend steeply toward the tree, which is two feet in diameter. The spring lies twenty feet southeast of this oak tree.

From the spring, besides the path eastward toward Polack Brook (and on to Mary Crose's Mountain, a berrypickers' encampment that will be described in a later chapter), another route probably headed northwest to connect to a path that went down the mountainside through a "wood slashin'," hitting Berme Road about three-tenths of a mile northeast of the kink in the road at Port Ben. This trail was used by day pickers ascending the mountain from the Rondout Valley. There was also a path to the spring from the top of the Jacob's Ladder, as well as the route from Panther Rock. Hank Green's Spring quenched the thirst of berrypickers from Mary Crose's, day pickers from the "slashin'" and Jacob's Ladder paths, and on occasion may have been the destination of a few pickers who'd wandered down this far from the Smiley Road.

Chapter 3

Of Horseshoes
& Home Brews

About fifty feet beyond the trail intersection on the Smiley Road, a clearing on the right-hand side marks the site of Nina Addis's cabin and store. The ground here is terraced, with three distinct levels discernible: Closest to the road was the storefront, on the lowest level, and to the left was an unenclosed flat where empty berry crates were stacked. Behind, on the second level, was a lean-to, open on one side, where crates full of huckleberries were stored. On the highest level, maybe twenty-five or thirty feet from the road, were the sleeping quarters, connected to the store by a roofed walkway that gave the impression of a single large structure. Nina's cabin was the only one besides Blacky's that was still standing when I passed through here in 1962. Remnants of it remained, in deteriorating condition, as late as 1977.

In the roadway in front of the store, the men and grown boys would often gather in the evening to pitch horseshoes. Nina was about the only woman who would join them in the game. "Ma, she played horseshoes just as good as they did, and a lot better," says Hype. Halfway between here and the trail junction previously described is the section of road where all the children would play Duck on the Rock. Hype also pointed out for me a small, semicircular flat on the south side of the road, a little to the Ellenville side of the trail junction, that still bears evidence of its many years of use as a parking spot for Nina's '29 Buick.

When Nina and her two children had first come to the Four-Mile Post in the early 1930s, they settled a couple of minutes west of this location. Nina's earliest cabin was on the right-hand side as you come up the mountain from Ellenville, immediately before the path that now leads over the rocks to the hunters' cabin on the south side of the road. It had been constructed at home and carried up on the back of a pickup truck. A small, home-made trailer was towed behind the truck and set down across the road on the left, a couple of yards closer to Ellenville. The trailer served as the store, and just to the right of it, as you face the site from the road, was a lean-to that served as the kitchen area. Behind are some flat rocks that were used as a sort of table. The cabin itself was moved a couple of years later and became Nina's storefront at her permanent location.

Although the memory of Nina Addis will always be most intimately associated with her many years here at the Four-Mile Post, it should not be forgotten that her early childhood summers from the age of about seven to nine were passed at the camp on the Stony Kill. She also told me of having spent perhaps a week or two there one summer in the mid to late 1920s, several years before coming to the Four-Mile Post. For a mattress, she and her husband, Lawrence, lay poles down on the ground or floor and picked sweet fern, which they piled on top, followed by blankets.

At the Four-Mile Post, Nina had an old hand-cranked Victrola that she'd occasionally play for the entertainment of her pickers. That most of the entertainment here was provided live by the berrypickers themselves, however, is borne out by the story Nina told me of a woman who camped here during the later period, from just after the War through most of the 1950s. This woman had a habit of walking in her sleep, or in her common-law husband's sleep, at any rate, and trying out a different cabin nearly every night, I suppose to see which had the most comfortable quarters. Her husband never seemed to mind at first, since she never left his side until he was in a deep coma, which generally occurred as soon as the last nightcap had been put away. But it seems that he would occasionally awaken late during the night and, missing his companion, would rouse much of the camp by loudly calling out her name. This same audience would then hear his wife's voice from somewhere about hollering, "Oh, shut up and go back to sleep," which request was dutifully obeyed. And by daybreak the couple were faithfully united, neither one of them (to all outward appearances) having any recollection of the night's events.

Later I learned from others the identity of this free spirit. I was also informed that she was a good homemaker and had some modest musical talent, with one favorite song that became something of a trademark. Alice Skiff Conklin told me, "E——- was a good cook. And she was clean—didn't she always tie her hair up in a white rag or something? Yes, she was a clean cook. And I don't care how drunk she was, her house was spotless." Fred Conklin said, "She'd blow that mouth organ and sing that song. That's all she knew. E——- had that song down pat. She'd be goin' from one shack to the other, she had visited somebody's camp down below, whoever she visited that night. You laid there and you'll hear her goin' down the road, singin':

> *All around the water tank, waitin' for a train,*
> *A thousand miles away from home, jus' sleepin' in the rain,*
> *I hadn't got a nickel, not a penny could I show,*
> *He said 'Get off, you railroad bum,' and he slammed that*
> *boxcar door.*

And we'll say: 'Yep, E——-'s drunk.'"

A man named Ernest ("Jerk") Vandermark was up here at the Four-Mile Post for many years and used to hang around outside Nina's store. He became a first-class nuisance to her, occasionally pilfering miscellaneous items, including even articles of clothing hung out to dry. He sometimes slept outdoors on the rocks nearby or even in the middle of the road. All this according to Nina, who related that once the two of them got into a fight, which ended when she broke his arm. Hype Addis told me it was his nose, not his arm, that got broken, and that "Jerk" fled down toward Decker's but eventually returned to the Four-Mile Post. He was ostracized for a time by the others at the camp, who simply ignored him thereafter, with Nina refusing to buy his berries. But eventually he was tolerated once again, and he ended up staying on nearly till Nina's last year. Vandermark lived for a number of summers in the same wooden cabin used previously by Blacky and by Mike the Polack. He is suspected of being responsible for setting fire first to one, then another of the shacks that had been abandoned, over a period of time during the 1950s.

Hype told me of another incident at the Four-Mile Post, when Jerk Vandermark got into an argument with Ben Slover and came back later and started pounding him on the head with a cake of soap tied up inside a woman's stocking. This occurred in the early fifties, when Hype was at the camp to buy berries. A year or two previous to this, when Hype had his store down at the Two-Mile Post and measured berries for Grover Perkins, Jerk Vandermark had paid him an unwelcome visit, which Hype returned with interest:

> *Kid Dayton and I used to go out picking huckleberries every morning, the two of us. We'd get back home around twelve o'clock, something like that, sometimes one o'clock, with our pails full. This day when I came back, I had two, three cases of empty bottles out there by the store, beer bottles and soda bottles, and they were all busted to pieces. And a little girl, that baby-sat for the Williams, next door, told me that Jerk Vandermark came down with two, three buddies, half-drunk, and just busted all the bottles.*

> *So that afternoon when Grover Perkins came up, I asked him if I could ride up to the Four-Mile with him, I drive right up to the Four-Mile with him and there goes Jerk with a cigar in his mouth, bottle of beer*

in his hands. I hit him right in the jaw and when he fell, first he hit the mirror on the car, then the door handle, then the runnin' board, then the stones, and time he got down to the stones, he laid there, he just didn't bother to get back up. So then he agreed to pay for the bottles, the deposit. My mother took it out of his pay, every time he picked huckleberries she took so much out for me, till it was paid for.

Hype recalls the following experience, which he places in August 1936, when he was eight years old. A number of pickers had spent the day over to the Fly Brook and Lake Awosting, where the swampberries (high-bush berries) were ripe:

We were going over to the Fly Brook to pick up the huckleberry pickers to bring them back to the Four-Mile Post. It was my father Lawrence Addis, my sister June, Herman Countryman, and myself was in the front seat of the truck, which was a new Ford pickup. And meanwhile four or five boys had come up from Ellenville, they were fifteen- or sixteen-year-old boys, they wanted to go back to Awosting Lake. They were summer residents just going for a walk, and they took a ride with us. After we left the Four-Mile Post, between the Four and the Five, at about the highest part of the road, Dad stopped quick and Herman got out and killed a big rattlesnake. It was huge, it stretched all the way across the road, it had to be at least a five-footer. And he put the snake into a big huckleberry pail, the snake was dead but it was still moving around inside the pail. And the boys were so scared they never went nowhere, they wouldn't ride in back with the snake, so they rode the running boards and the tailgate till they got back to the Four-Mile Post and went right straight down that mountain.

Hype told me a story concerning a huckleberry picker named Julius, who'd been coming up to the Four-Mile Post for many years, and another picker known as Bad Bill:

In the summer of 1938 Julius and a man by the name of Bad Bill camped together. Julius was a very quiet camper and Bad Bill would get on a tear once in a while. So they got into a couple of little arguments during the summer, drinking this and that. This one night Julius come in, he had a couple of drinks, and Bad Bill was in the camp, throwing all of Julius's stuff out. Well, Julius went inside and kicked him out through the side of the camp, right through the tarpaper wall. Meanwhile, Bad Bill pulled a knife and Harry and Roy Alexander took the knife away from him.

Apparently Bad Bill's reputation was not confined to the Four-Mile Post. Florence and Hazel Slover, sisters who camped as children at the Five-Mile Post, also remember "Bad Bill Monroe" as someone who'd make everyone nervous whenever he'd show up there. "They'd talk about him. Everybody'd be scared of him. They used to say he went to jail a lot of times and then, when they heard, they'd say, 'Oh my God, *Bad Bill Monroe is out of jail!*'"

Bad Bill left the Four-Mile Post and camped the rest of the summer of '38 at Sam's Point. But the next year, the year of the big fire, he was back at the Four-Mile Post.

"Bad Bill was a kind of a sneaky guy," Hype continued:

He always carried a knife on him. Now he was hanging around with another family up there. He was acting like he was very good friends with everybody, including Julius. Julius always left his stuff packed in the mountain. He had a lot of weaved baskets, and all his gear was stored during the winter, from year to year. So 1939 was the fire, and everybody fought fire. This one day, Julius just disappeared. Never heard from him since. And every bit of his things was left in the camp. He camped alone then.

He's there someplace in that mountain, everybody knows. He might have fallen in a crevice, but people always had that suspicion that Bad Bill had done him in.

Bernie "Hype" Addis, on a visit to the author's cabin,
June 1992.

I asked Hype to tell me some more about the 1939 fire,
which was one of the many blazes set by pickers to improve the
berry crop (and the only one I know of to get out of hand and
threaten the camps themselves). "The fire came right up to the
rocks around the campground," Hype said. "John Addis, the
forest ranger at that time with the CC [Civilian Conservation
Corps] guys, he wanted everybody to move off the Four-Mile
Post—he said it was up to them if they wanted to move or not.
But they all stayed and they all built backfires. They all
backfired *to* the fire, that's what stopped it."

Nina Addis told me her memories of the same blaze:

*Yes, I can remember that: At the time that fire was,
the fire was moving towards the Four-Mile Post. The
fire was in up the tops of the trees, the blaze was all
over. The CCC boys were there, fire wardens were there,*

47

people had been picked up from Ellenville to help fight the fire, and some of the pickers went out to help fight the fire. The Van Leuven family had a store there, and they moved out. They went down the mountain. In my store, I had such a supply of huckleberries, in the hundreds of dollars, and my store full, that I took my car and moved it out on the rocks, and put most of my possessions into the car. It was a big flat rock, I thought I could backfire. So I stayed there. Most of the other pickers did too. They stayed pat. They thought if I could stay there that they could also stay there.

Hype related a story I recognized as one I'd heard from Nina some years earlier but had neglected to record. This occurred about the early 1950s and concerns a man of about fifty years, a berrypicker named Slim who took ill and died on the mountain. "That same day that he was sick, he complained of pains in his side and the rangers were up in there, they were checking out their fire lines and things, they came back out, they had their jeep, and they offered to drive him back down the mountain to the hospital and he didn't want to go, and he died that night of a busted appendix. They all stayed in to Mary Quick's camp and they held his hands, and he went through his death throb right there; they held him right in their arms and he died."

During his last several years as a buyer, in the late 1950s, Hype couldn't always market all his berries fresh; so he would freeze the excess, twenty pounds to a can, and then sell them to bakeries through a jobber during the winter. Before freezing the berries he'd pour them out in front of an electric fan to eliminate some of the stray leaves. Bakers would usually dump their frozen huckleberries into a tub of water before use, to thaw them and enable some of the twigs, leaves, and worms to float to the top.

Berry rakes were strongly frowned upon; few people used them, and then generally while picking unseen. Rakes were considered too rough on the bushes, denuding them of leaves and unripe berries (which thus became mixed with the rake-user's harvest). The pickers used metal pails or wicker baskets or something called a "knock-a-box" to collect their berries. Many of the wicker baskets were woven locally by berrypickers themselves or by other native craftspeople. The "knock-a-box" may have been peculiar to the people at the Two-Mile Post: It consisted of a cardboard box perhaps twice the size of a shoebox, with the front end partially removed with a concave, semicircular cut. A wooden cross member was inserted about six inches from the front, serving as a hand grip. The box was thus "worn" on the forearm, with the free hand used to shake berries into the box, while the branch or bush was kept steady by the curved cut-out of the box's front.

Until about the time of the War, a few people at the Smiley Road camps still used home-made wooden berry boxes: These had shoulder straps and were worn in much the same way as a backpack. As the picker's basket or pail filled up, it would be emptied into this box, which held about twenty to thirty quarts. The berry box had been standard equipment in the days before the Smiley Road, when many pickers climbed up from the valley on day trips and needed greater carrying capacity and convenience than a hand basket offered. Because of the distances typically walked by berrypickers at Sam's Point, boxes were still in use there through the 1950s.

Although serious pickers averaged perhaps twenty to forty quarts a day, there were also many who merely picked enough to buy their day's food and drink. Meals at the huckleberry camps were heated or cooked using various means: A few households enjoyed the luxury of a kerosene cookstove, while most cooked outdoors with a wood fire, using stoves fashioned from old barrels or a car's fuel tank. Down at the Two-Mile Post, Fred Conklin informed me, ninety percent of the families simply used old makeshift grates or grills over an open fire and didn't worry too much about the bottoms of the pots and pans getting dirty.

I gathered from what Nina had told me that her husband, Lawrence, whom she divorced in 1955, was a wild sort, a gambler, who never spent much time at the berry camps. "It was too mild for him" up there, she had said. "There was no excitement." I also learned that Lawrence had had substantial underworld connections and had earned much of his living in the bootleg trade. I never asked for details, out of respect for Nina and also because I supposed that her former husband had little to tell me about the mountain, if in fact the man were still alive. But when I learned from others in September 1982 that he was living in Tampa, Florida and that he might indeed have stories to tell, curiosity got the better of me, and I resolved to look him up on my annual hitchhiking trip to the Keys, two months later.

I phoned Lawrence Addis from a booth in Fort Myers Beach and identified myself and my reason for calling; he agreed to see me. On the morning of November 14 I approached his very modest cottage on Waters Avenue in Sulphur Springs. In the driveway was an enormous red Cadillac. On the front porch sat a tall, heavy-set man of eighty years whose demeanor suggested someone still very much in command, but perhaps grown tired of life. I was a bit earlier than expected, though I had forewarned him that my method of travel was one that did not allow for precise planning.

As I walked toward the door he looked up and inquired, "Mr. Fried?" When I replied in the affirmative, he immediately reached for the telephone extension by his side and announced, "Mr. Fried is here." Within seconds we were joined by a tall, rugged-looking man in his fifties who sat silently in our company as Lawrence and I engaged in conversation. After ten minutes or so, apparently satisfied that I was not someone who'd been contracted to settle some old grievance, Addis turned for the first time to his silent companion and said simply, "O.K., you can go," or something to that effect.

We talked for about an hour, and I have to say I liked the man. He seemed increasingly at ease and willingly answered my questions when he could provide answers, relating for me an anecdote or two worth retelling. Neither was he shy about acknowledging his old Mafia ties. He confided that although he'd been well-connected, as an ethnic outsider he never was part of an inner circle. And he'd been beaten up a few times, he said. But he claimed he still had connections, if ever he needed to use them.

When we neared the end of our exchange, he said that now, having answered my inquiries, he had a question of his own. He prevailed upon me to be truthful and hold back nothing:

"What do they say about me back home?" he asked. I replied that people said he'd been a bootlegger.

"True," he answered. I told him of something else I had heard said.

"No," he replied. "I sometimes provided women for my business associates, as a favor, but I never made money off them."

After my return from Florida later in the fall of 1982, I sent Lawrence Addis a Christmas card, which he didn't, however, acknowledge. On August 4, 1985, Lawrence blew his brains out. I learned about it from the Deckers on Rock Haven Road the next day; as it happens, I was on my way to visit Nina at the time. When my indirect reference to the event failed to elicit an informed response, I asked, rather surprised, "You mean you haven't heard about Lawrence?"

"Did the Devil take him?" inquired Nina.

"He took himself," I answered.

Hype Addis told me of his father's involvement in a number of bootlegging operations. These were both during and after the Prohibition era, for business connections, distribution networks, and people's habits were slow to disappear even after alcoholic beverages had become legal again. Typically, Lawrence would be the brains in a two- or three-man operation, the still being hidden inside some old barn or vacant boarding house that the men had rented. His partners would be the "cooks" engaged in actual manufacture of the alcohol, while Lawrence would deliver to them the necessary sugar and yeast, the kerosene or fuel oil, and empty five-gallon cans. Lawrence would then distribute the finished product along a route to stores, hotels, and other customers, collecting payment. On the mountain he'd bring it only to the Four-Mile Post. Hype, Lawrence, and others whom I've spoken to absolutely denied something I'd previously been told, namely, that during the 1930s and '40s two stills operated in close proximity to the huckleberry camps, one of them supposedly near the Two-Mile Post.

Hype tells me none of his father's stills lasted very long before being found by the police, but his father and the other partners would always get wind of the busts in advance and were never implicated; soon Lawrence would be setting up shop in another location. Sometime during the War years, Lawrence abandoned direct involvement in the manufacturing process and used his Mob connections to purchase quantities of alcohol in the Rutherford, New Jersey area, for distribution in and around Ulster County.

Whichever the source, the alcohol, generally 180 to 190 proof, would first be cut with fifty percent water and colored with a little burnt sugar before being sold retail. "Sometimes," Hype said, "Pop would empty a bottle of store-bought whiskey into the can for good luck." Hype knows of only two occasions when his father got caught red-handed. These both occurred about 1953 or '54 and only involved possession of small amounts of illicit alcohol. About this time, Lawrence found more respectable ways to earn a living. For all his years on the shady side of the law, Lawrence never served time behind bars.

Hype related for me a little drama he shared with his father, that took place on the mountain:

> *This was during the early part of the War, the 1940s, Dad bought beer off somebody in Ellenville that had cases and cases of beers stored in the old Pepsi-Cola factory [the former Sun Ray bottling plant and present factory outlet, on Berme Road just outside of Ellenville]. This was manufactured, it was Charlie Evans Ale, the beer was actually a legit company in Kingston. But when they hit Prohibition they had to*

close down. So this guy apparently had part of the company, this guy's share was a few thousand cases of beer. It laid there for years and years and Pop used to go up there and buy, you know, ten cases at a time, whatever he could get in the back of the truck. And he used to take it to the mountain. And this beer had all yeast sediments on the bottom, but it was still good beer.

On the way up, there was revenue men comin' up behind us, and when we got to the Three-Mile Post the ol' '29 Buick was steamin', and we had to pour water over the radiator to cool it down, meanwhile Pop stayed to cool it down and made sure to block the road, and I run from the Three-Mile to the Four-Mile, warning people that he's gonna stop and give each one a case of beer on the way up. And so when he got to the store there was no beer left. Then after the revenue men went back down the mountain, Pop had to go back down, pick all his beer back up.

Although this of course occurred after Prohibition, the family's store at the Four-Mile Post was not licensed to sell alcoholic beverages. But there was nothing illegal about simply making a "beer run" as a favor to people along the road who'd supposedly laid out money in advance.

During the years when Lawrence was selling moonshine, Nina's little store on the mountain was always well-supplied with strong drink. Toward the end of the day, as some of the pickers got a little sluggish in their movements, Nina's pint bottles would tend to mellow out to sixty proof or so from the morning high of ninety. After the War, Nina simply stocked store-bought wine and beer, which she'd mark up slightly for resale.

During the final years, when there were only several berrypickers left at the Four-Mile Post, they would usually pool their berries as soon as there was enough to purchase a bottle or two of wine. This would occur around nine o'clock in the morning, about the time Nina was getting up, and was known as the "first run." There were usually three or four "runs" a day. Nina always had a free cup of coffee for the pickers in the morning. She'd start the week with a fresh pot, and each day she'd add a little more grounds. By the end of the week the pot would be about half full of grounds, and she'd dump it out and start over again.

Both Nina and Hype told me that revenue men would make their appearance at the Four-Mile Post every so often, generally once each summer. But you could spot them a mile away by their fine dress, and up close by the lack of calluses on their hands. So when they'd ask to buy a drink, Nina would simply tell them that she had nothing for sale, and the matter would be closed. Hype didn't say whether they ever availed themselves of his mother's free coffee, which by the end of the week must have been at least as strong as the beverages that were kept hidden from view.

Nina was born December 21, 1907, in Napanoch, the only child of Albert Quick and Elizabeth Crawford Quick. Her maternal grandmother was Mary Rose Crawford, a sister of Catharine Rose Countryman (later Markle), who was the mother of Bill Countryman. During Nina's last few years on the mountain, after the 1955 flood, the following are believed to have made up her final group of berrypickers: Art Countryman, Jerk Vandermark, and brothers Carl ("Timmy") and Ernie Sandstrom, all of whom probably stayed only through the summer of '56 (the Sandstrom brothers were born in Sweden in the first several years of this century and came to the United States as youths; they began camping at the Four-Mile Post after the War and may have done a little day picking now and then during 1957); Herman and Oscar Countryman, with the latter's common-law wife, Evelyn; and Rodney Smith, a friend, neighbor, and sometime employer of Bill Countryman, who lived during the year on the old New Paltz-Wawarsing Turnpike. The Countrymen[1] utilized the cabin that had formerly belonged to Mary Quick. By all accounts, Oscar and

---

[1] I've adopted the commonly heard plural form of this name, rendered as Country*men* (rather than Country*mans*).

Ernie Vandermark, Nina Addis, and friends, Four-Mile Post, 1940.

Evelyn were among her very last companions on the day Nina closed down her store and berrying operation forever.

Nina lived all her adult life in and about the hamlet of Granite, during the months of the year when she was not up on the Smiley Road. From about 1952 she resided in the only house she herself ever owned, a small frame dwelling on the southeast side of Stony Kill Road, nine-tenths of a mile northeast of its junction with Upper Granite Road. Here is where I met Nina Addis and here I returned every year to visit and to hear her many stories of life and times at the Four-Mile Post. My last visit to her was in the late summer of 1987. She was in good form and regaled me and a guest I'd brought with a few bawdy tales I'd never heard from her before. "I wish I'd brought my tape recorder," I said at one point. She assured me that the only reason I was hearing these stories was that I *didn't* have a recorder going.

Nina passed away on December 7 of that year, two weeks short of her eightieth birthday.

Chapter 4

The Four-Mile Post
to Polack Swamp

About a hundred feet farther along the Smiley Road past the site of Nina's store, there's a flat area on the left side of the road, just past a bit of a ravine. On this flat stood a large cabin occupied in the 1930s by brothers Roy and Harry Alexander and their families. Frank Quick told me this cabin was once struck by a bolt of lightning that traveled through the cookstove and blew the stove lid into the air while the folks sat inside. The Quicks' cabin was struck simultaneously, with ground currents apparently traveling between the two.

Directly across the road from the Alexanders, on the same side as Nina's, we come to the ruins of Blacky's cabin. This was in good condition until destroyed in late 1981 or the early part of '82. During the year or two before its destruction, the state park folks had told me openly that the cabin would have to come down, because of its status as an "attractive nuisance" (the first part of the term referring to its tendency to attract undesirables), a rape having reportedly occurred there at some time in the past. It has always seemed to me that this line of reasoning should qualify many a motel room and perhaps the occasional suburban bedroom for demolition as well. At any rate, the actual destruction of the cabin is supposed to have been caused, not by the park people, but by persons who'd been kicked out of the cabin and had returned to vent their wrath on a suitably passive victim. It was an act of unconscionable vandalism by whoever the perpetrators.

This cabin was formerly the site of the Van Leuven store. The Van Leuvens were hard-working people, and the berrypicking exploits of one daughter in particular were legendary. Hype Addis told me Ethel Van Leuven could sometimes be discovered in the bushes literally surrounded by pails full of huckleberries, which her father, Winslow, would carry out for her, replacing them with more empties. Ray Quick of Walden told me he once timed her by the second hand of his watch as she picked a quart of berries in one minute. Winslow and Bertha Van Leuven brought much of their berry harvest directly to the kitchens of the Minnewaska and Mohonk mountain houses. Ethel and her brother Roger inform me that the family's first summer at the Four-Mile Post was 1934, several months before the birth of their younger brother Richard. Their store and living quarters were built in large part with old dynamite boxes that Winslow collected when he was employed in the construction of Route 52, which crosses the mountain between Ellenville and Walker Valley. The boxes were taken apart and the short boards used as siding for the Van Leuven cabin, the studs consisting of narrow tree trunks placed relatively close together.

Blacky was born in Austria during the early to mid 1880s. Hoping to pursue a career as a botanist, he was forced by economic circumstances to terminate his studies at the age of about nineteen and emigrate to the United States. Here he found employment for many years working on barges in the port of New York. In later years Blacky worked as head of a crew of dishwashers at a fancy restaurant in the Wall Street area of Manhattan. He began spending summers in the Shawangunk Mountains late in the second decade of this century, staying at the "German Camp" at Sam's Point. In 1919, when the State was preparing to erect the High Point fire tower, Blacky was hired with two or three other men to carry sections of steel up to the site. The steel was hauled up from Ellenville with horses as far as the latter could go, and the men worked about a month bringing it up to the top of the cliff. I believe the route used was via the Smiley Road and that the horses were able to traverse the pathway south from the vicinity of the Three-Mile Post, nearly to the foot of High Point.

Blacky's nickname derived from his dark hair and rather swarthy complexion. He and a couple of others from the German Camp moved over to the Smiley Road and took up residence on the Beaver Creek, shortly after the cabins at the Three-Mile Post had been destroyed by authorities. Soon Blacky and his companions were also compelled to leave. Then Blacky moved up to the Four-Mile Post, where initially he settled into a vacant shack.

The foregoing biographical information was provided to me by Blacky's longtime friend and companion, Mr. Meinrad Broghammer. Meinrad, born in Germany in 1901, was a mason by trade. He began making occasional summertime visits to the mountain about 1940, joining Blacky at the Four-Mile Post, where Meinrad recalls there being about fifty people in those

Blacky (left, foreground) and Meinrad outside Mary Quick's cabin, ca. 1956.

days. In their early years here, Blacky and he would appropriate one or another vacant cabin for their summer sojourns. Through his friendship with the Van Leuvens, Blacky was able to obtain possession of their large, multi-roomed structure after that family moved over to Sam's Point. Blacky's cabin was built in the early fifties, in part using materials from the old Van Leuven store and family quarters.

At this point it becomes necessary for me to correct a common misconception: Although Blacky spent more time at their cabin than Meinrad did, at least during the 1950s and '60s, and was the better known of the pair, it was in fact Meinrad, not Blacky, who actually built the cabin, working weekends over the course of three months. "Blacky couldn't hit a nail straight," Meinrad told me with a laugh. The latter's creative handiwork is elsewhere evident in his taxidermy and in his two rock paintings: a black bear near the Five-Mile Post and a black panther near the bend of the cliff line 650 yards along the trail from High Point toward the Four-Mile Post. This panther lies north of the path, immediately before the latter dips to cross the first little swale. (But the toothy reptile, now badly faded, that adorns a rock farther northeast along this same trail was not his, insists Meinrad, who told me it predated his own arrival.)

Blacky and Meinrad were summertime visitors to the Four-Mile Post during and even long after Nina Addis's last years here. Meinrad told me that he himself picked berries only for his own consumption, preserving thirty or forty quarts each year for winter use. Blacky did sell some berries to the Van Leuvens and, later, to Nina, until the road washed out and outside buyers could no longer visit the Four-Mile Post. But the two men were essentially vacationers, not berrypickers, and thus were not part of the tightly knit group that made up the last commercial berrypicking community on the upper Smiley Road.

Meinrad praised his friend as someone much in tune with nature and described for me how Blacky had tamed a doe up at their camp. The doe had a young one back in the bushes, but she never brought it out. Blacky would call, "Nonny, Nonny,

Nonny" or "Nunzy, Nunzy, Nunzy" and the doe would come right out, in the daytime, and eat out of Blacky's hand. But the deer would never let anyone touch her. He also tamed a snowshoe hare. He would call, "Hansel, Hansel, Hansel," and the hare would come right to his feet. "One time," says Meinrad, "it was a hot day and I had made berries and I put it down in front of the shack where the shade was. And we were eating there. When I looked, the rabbit was sitting right in the berries. I had almost to grab him before he would leave. I said 'You S.O.B., you wouldn't have to go inside, you can eat from *out*side!'"

Meinrad also related the following tale: "Blacky and I, we were in bed, about ten o'clock. Had the lights out, but we were still a little talking. And then we heard a screech owl. She must have been sitting up there on top of our shack. All at once, on top of the roof. . . [here Meinrad imitated the sound of an animal springing up on top of the roof]. . . and on the other side, down. I always had a flashlight with me, handy. I jumped out of the bed, mit the flashlight, and seen it going away. I could not swear what it was—but it could not be anything else than a bobcat. No raccoon could do it; nothing like that can make a jump that high. I jumped out and I seen it running away."

One nice spring morning about 1965, Blacky and Meinrad arrived at their cabin to find that a bumblebee queen had a nest inside and was entering and exiting through a hole in the side of the window, in the northwest corner of the cabin. "We didn't want to get stung and we didn't want to disturb her," Meinrad told me. Meinrad caught the bee in a paper bag and carried it all the way to the highest point in the road, before the descent into the Stony Kill gorge toward the Five-Mile Post. "I told Blacky, 'You stay here and watch if he comes back.' When I came back, he said, 'The bumblebee's home before you.'" Meinrad caught the bee once more and walked with it clear to the Five-Mile Post, and this time the bee got lost, "because of the high hill in between," surmises Meinrad.

Blacky and Meinrad's cabin was the scene of much activity during the fire of 1964, the last big blaze on the mountain.

Meinrad told me his recollections:

> *Many times I worked up at Woodstock. So I came down there and I seen the fire, I says "I'm going up." I seen the fire from far away. The Salvation Army had a camp there [in our cabin] at the Four-Mile Post. And they gave out coffee and stuff like that. I had in mind to stay there, you know, but when I see it, so I didn't bother. But I spoke to them. They gave me coffee. Then I left and I went down the mountain.*

According to Meinrad, the fire approached, but did not cross, the swale and water hole just northeast of the camp. But between the Four- and Five-Mile posts it did cross over the road before being brought under control.

Blacky died about 1975-78. He always maintained an apartment in New York City, but his heart and home were in the Shawangunk Mountains. He made summertime visits to his cabin practically to the time of his death at the age of ninety-three. When summer came, "you couldn't hold him in New York," Meinrad told me. Meinrad himself made occasional camping trips to the Four-Mile Post until he discovered his cabin in ruins in July of 1982. He wrote to me, "Well my dear friend, nothing lasts forever and the clouds now travel over it."

In the summer of 1962 I met a companion of Blacky's named Hans, who was living at the Four-Mile Post in Nina's old quarters. This Hans, I have since learned, was industrious in a rather eccentric way. Near a cranberry bog a few hundred yards northeast of Blacky's cabin, Hans once spent a week digging out a sizeable hollow, "so the deer would have a place to swim." Nearby was a miniature cave formed by an overhanging rock, under which Hans would hide some of his personal belongings before coming down from the mountain. Hans also worked about three weeks constructing a somewhat redundant trail, "going down and up and down and up," as Meinrad described it, from near Napanoch Point all the way to the High Point fire tower, which trail Hans marked with tar or black paint. On a smooth outcrop alongside the Smiley Road, at

Blacky and Meinrad's cabin, 1963.

the trail's northern terminus, he chiseled the words "HAMLOCK TRAIL TO TOWER." This inscription (with the *A* in the first word later corrected to a crude *E*) is visible today, two minutes' walk from the horseshoe curve that takes the road up above the cliff line.

The inscription is accompanied by a few black arrows pointing along the rocks, but Hans's trail immediately loses itself amongst the crackerberry bushes. After dropping off the cliff and crossing somewhere through the hemlock forests and swamps of the upper Beaver Creek, it reappears just north of the fire tower site, where it encounters the footpath that leads south toward High Point from the Three-Mile Post. Hans's trail follows this path briefly and then continues for a short distance along the Fire Tower Road to the foot of another path, the one ascending northeastward to the tower site. At this point there is a rock with the words "HAMLOCK TRAIL TO THE NEW ROAD," marking the southwest terminus of Hans's trail.

I sought and found the cranberry bog that Meinrad described: The alternate branch of the trail to Decker's leaves the Smiley Road opposite Blacky's cabin and heads northeastward, dipping down past the site of the Alexanders' cabin to the spring and a little stone-lined well that supplied water to the Four-Mile Post, then bearing right, through the bushes, and gradually climbing to the rock outcrop on the other side of this swale. (On this outcrop was the shack where Julius and Bad Bill had camped together, one of only two cabins that stood across the swale from the road.) As one follows the path one sees a larger swale ahead, at the bottom of a slope, where the path dips down to a crossing place. Just beyond this larger swale is a row of tall trees. From here to the Smiley Road is a three or four minute walk, and the cranberry bog is about a hundred yards upstream in the swale. A little farther upstream, on the left, is a rift in the rocks that may or may not be Hans's storage place. I was unable to find any swimming pool for deer, but one may assume this would have filled in with mud and debris before very many years had passed.

We return to the Smiley Road and bid goodbye to the ruins of Blacky and Meinrad's cabin. Before we proceed on our way east, our eyes are drawn to some botanical anomalies in the form of a clump of lilac and an apple tree, planted by one or both of the men to beautify their front yard.

About twenty-five yards eastward along the road from Blacky's, on the same side, there's a rock outcrop alongside the road, and just above it, a grassy knoll on which another cabin was once located. Hype tells me this was occupied by an elderly man named Phil Damm, in the 1930s. There were other cabins to the rear, including one in which Blacky had sometimes camped in the years before his own cabin was built, according to Frank Quick.

Another ten yards or so farther, a shack once stood atop the mossy area on our right, on a knoll just above another outcrop. Hype remembers only that the man who lived here was named George, "and he had a finger missin'." There were no kids, just George and his wife. "He was skinny and she was fat. And she was always complainin' because he'd always bring her right straight home through the brush instead of the trail. After they was out pickin' huckleberries, he'd bushwhack his way all the way home."

Continuing eastward along the road for one minute, we come to a small outcrop on our right. A few yards farther, on the left, a driveway formerly left the road and gave access to a cabin some distance in the rear, in which lived a lay preacher and his wife. This cabin was about a minute's walk distant from Julius's shack. Hype told me the man was tall and skinny, with a long beard. He drove a Model A Ford and wore bib overalls. "This minister, when he was young, he was a lawyer," Hype related.

> *His wife had T.B. And he prayed that if his wife got better he would give up all his worldly goods and go to the teaching. And his wife got better and he did. I guess they were farmers after that.*
>
> *The minister, once a year, he'd get all us kids together, however many was here, and outdoors, at his cabin, he had all these little strings tied fast, with our names onto 'em, and we'd wind this string all up, up and down around the bushes, and time we'd get to the end of the string would be our little presents—candies, whatever it was in those days. We really all looked forward to it every summer.*

Another four minutes along our way a run of water crosses the road, where some swampberries grow. Nearby, on the right-hand side, a large Polish family camped for many years. The place has always been known as Polack Camp or Polack Swamp, and the stream that runs from here down the mountain to Foordmoor Road was sometimes called Polack Brook. The cabin itself stood about fifteen yards past the water crossing and the same distance from the road, at the upper edge of an outcrop.

The man of the family was known to all as Polack Joe, a name he is said to have invariably used when referring to himself. The other members of the family whose names I've been able to learn were two sons named Johnny and Mikey and a daughter Mary. Polack Joe was by all accounts a well-liked, colorful character whose speech bore the imprint of his origins in the Old Country. Joe was born sometime during the final two decades of the last century and was already on the mountain when Nina Addis first came up to the Four-Mile Post as an adult in the early 1930s. He picked berries for the Van Leuvens. His wife died about 1940, and the children, all grown by then, did not return to the mountain. Joe camped alone for about another two summers. During these last years, I'm told, he had a couple of porcupines as regular visitors who even slept inside the cabin with him as companions of a sort.

Two stories were related to me about Polack Joe. The first, from Ray Quick, was independently confirmed by Lawrence Addis. This incident is supposed to have occurred about 1930, along the road between Highland and Clintondale, where Joe and his family lived during most of the year. Joe had given a friend of his an old horse that Joe no longer had use for. According to Ray, who claimed to have heard the story straight from the horse's mouth (from Joe, that is), "The next winter Joe stopped by his friend's house to talk to him a few minutes, and he invited him in to dinner, and he said they had some nice meat on the table. His friend said to him, 'How ya like that meat, Joe?' Joe says, 'Him's good.' His friend said, 'Him's your horse!'"

The second story occurred sometime in the 1960s and concerns the circumstances that led to Joe's death. This tale was related by Rae Decker, who was living with George Decker by the pond above Rock Haven Road at the time these events took place. The berry business up on the Smiley Road was a thing of the past by then, even Nina Addis having left the mountain some years before. But Polack Joe, well into his seventies, had returned to the mountain alone for a few days of picking berries. According to Rae, Joe came down from the Four-Mile Post with a twelve-quart pail full of the most beautiful low-bush berries she had seen in years. Joe was limping somewhat, and she and George insisted on having a look at his foot. They discovered that Joe had tied a string around his toe, apparently to ease the pain of an ingrown toenail. Complications set in, and the loss of his toe was soon followed by the amputation of the entire leg.

Things went from bad to worse, and the doctors advised that the old man's remaining leg would have to be amputated as well. It was then that Polack Joe decided he'd had enough and that he would not be a burden to himself and others (his demise followed shortly after his refusal to undergo another operation): Said Joe, "I come into this world with two legs, and I'm goin' out with at least one."

Chapter 5

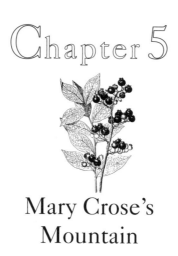

Mary Crose's Mountain

Forty or fifty feet beyond Polack Swamp, directly across from where Joe's cabin once stood, a road comes in from the left, at a point where the Smiley Road curves slightly rightward. The unwary tramper who takes the wrong fork here will soon be on his way down the mountainside toward Decker's Pond. This bulldozed pathway, which for the hiker essentially duplicates the footpath between Decker's and the Four-Mile Post, was reportedly built as a future fire access trail in the autumn of 1947, shortly after the conflagration that blackened much of the mountain from Sam's Point to Castle Point. During the second half of the 1950s, the road served to keep alive the final commercial berrying operation at the Four-Mile Post, after the route down to Ellenville had become nearly impassable.

Via a private driveway, through land no longer available for public access, the bottom of the fire trail connects to the upper end of Rock Haven Road, a dead-end public road that winds halfway up the mountain from its lower terminus near the Minnewaska Trail. In years past I had often heard the name Mary Crose's Mountain used in connection with the upper reaches of Rock Haven and had half-consciously rebelled against the term: It offended my geographic sensibilities in seeming to imply that this area was somehow something other than an integral part of Shawangunk Mountain. But finally my curiosity led me to start asking questions, and I learned of a distinct locus of commercial huckleberry picking, one that provided an important and readily accessible source of summertime employment for the folks around Kerhonkson and vicinity. At the center of this berrying operation was a woman whose name became a monument to industry, character, and benevolence among the people who knew and still remembered her.

Mary was born February 5, 1860, at Greenfield (now Greenfield Park), the daughter of Jacob Caston and Aba Jane Slater. Through her grandfather Thomas Slater, there came into her possession a considerable amount of land along the highest section of Rock Haven Road. In 1892 Mary Caston married Caleb Crose, who came with a large number of half-grown children from a prior marriage. Mary bore two children, Ethel and Art. The marriage apparently never flourished: Caleb would periodically go on a drunk and stay away for a time, then be physically threatening or abusive upon his return. He soon either left for good or was kicked out, and Mary took in a "boarder," a German by the name of Charles Fisher, who helped raise Mary's two children, and with whom she maintained a relationship until death parted them.

Mary had suffered a childhood disease or injury of some kind that resulted in a recurring infection in one of her legs and a number of surgical procedures. In middle age the leg was amputated. It is said that some of Mary's former fellow employees at Mohonk took up a collection that helped pay for a wooden leg. This was held in place by straps and had a compartment in which Mary would hide money. A common prank involved her son, Art, hiding the leg on her.

I've been unable to learn for certain the nature of the original affliction that ultimately resulted in the loss of her natural limb. But a story persists that it was due to a rattlesnake bite that occurred while picking berries as a child, or to some injury sustained while avoiding a rattlesnake. I heard this tale from old Ernie Smith of Napanoch, who had close ties to the family, and from Mary's granddaughter Loretta Mc Clain, who remembers hearing the story from a hired hand who'd boarded with Mary and who afterward lived for many years with Loretta's family during her youth. I accompanied Loretta on a visit to her aunt Ethel Crose Decker, Mary's daughter, at the New Paltz Nursing Home, when Ethel was eighty-eight years of age. Ethel denied the rattlesnake story. But Loretta confided that her aunt's memory had been failing seriously, and that she'd contradicted some of her own statements regarding her mother, made on earlier occasions.

The nearest estimate Loretta and Ethel could make concerning the date of Mary's operation derives from something Ethel had recalled from childhood: Soon after the surgery, before Mary had been fitted with a wooden leg, she was unable to stand at a table to knead dough. And so the dough was placed on a kitchen chair, which was the right height for Ethel to perform the task. Loretta and her aunt had calculated that this would have been when Ethel was about eight years old, in 1902.

In 1894 Mary purchased from her grandfather the farm acreage at the upper end of Rock Haven Road that was to be her home for most of her years thereafter. Mary Crose's house stood until recently, on the left-hand side as you ascend the road, about three hundred yards above the power line crossing. The house was built in two sections having roof lines perpendicular to one another. The older portion had rafters of logs and was the first encountered as one approached the house from below. It may have been built by Mary, at the time she acquired the property. The second, more southerly portion was quite likely added about the early 1910s. Mary kept about ten dairy cows, which must have been an important source of income along with what she earned per quart for measuring berries.

As I talked with the people who had known Mary Crose, a picture emerged of a tall, robust woman, hard-working almost to a fault, sober and strong-willed, big-hearted and generous. Minnie Purcell, who came to work for Mary as a live-in helper at the age of perhaps thirteen or fourteen, not long after Mary's marriage, always talked of Mary Crose as her "second mother," according to Minnie's daughter-in-law Agnes Otis. Ernie Smith called her "a fine lady." Nellie Decker, whose father-in-law, Dan Decker, was the husband of Mary's sister Ella, told me, "Mary's house was home to everyone."

Those who knew anything about Mary Crose were unanimous in proclaiming her a marvelous cook, whose kitchen, pantry, and cellar were always stocked with a fabulous array of edibles. Her granddaughter Loretta told me of hearing that the visitor who dropped by her house was never permitted to leave without being served a meal: There were cakes and pies and puddings, as well as quantities of bananas and muskmelons, which issued forth uncannily from Mary's cellar at unexpected times of the year. Harry Lane (born 1899), who first picked huckleberries at Mary Crose's when barely in his teens, told me, "She was sort of a magician I guess you'd call her, 'cause every time you stopped in, you never knew where all the food came from."

The first location associated in the memories of old people with Mary's huckleberry business was somewhat lower on the road, near the former town landfill, just below where Shaft Road branches off from Rock Haven toward the Stony Kill Falls. I've had contradictory accounts as to which side of Rock Haven Road the house and pickers' cabins were on. Here there were about five or six shanties and perhaps twenty-five to forty berrypickers, most of whom camped, but a few of whom only came up to pick during the day. The Ulster County Deed Record shows this land was never owned by Mary Crose: It was bought by Mary's brother William in 1906 and retained until June 1913, when it was sold by William to his brother Arthur. The cabins were apparently thus on Willy's property, yet a few of the people I'd talked to (now deceased) had referred to this location as the "old Mary Crose house." Although Mary seems to have measured huckleberries down here for a number of years, it seems unlikely that she would actually have resided in the house of her younger brother, years after having acquired her own substantial acreage farther up the road—especially considering her strong, independent personality and what may be inferred from both local and family traditions concerning the character of her brother Willy.

Mary was never a berry buyer in her own right; she measured the berries that the pickers brought in and turned them over to her sister's husband, Dan Decker (1855-1934), who marketed them in Poughkeepsie, and to Abe Kelder, who had a summer hotel in the valley. According to Mary's daughter, Ethel, for a time Russel Van Etten had a little store nearby for the berrypickers' convenience. Mary herself would sometimes fill orders for perishable foods.

Sometime about the autumn of 1912, brother Willy is reported to have burned his own house down, hoping to collect a hefty payment from the insurance company. Although the story of Willy Caston's caper derives from several sources, the most interesting particulars about the escapade come via Lou Quick (born 1902), who, with his brother Ray, had been baby-sat by Mary's daughter as early as about 1905. Lou told me that Willy prevailed upon his brother-in-law Dan Decker to help move furniture, canned goods, winter roots, and so forth out of the house beforehand, a clever precaution designed to minimize substantive loss, but having the tendency to look suspicious when the investigators come around. This accomplished, a Caston daughter was supposedly requested by the man of the house to do the honors during the latter's convenient absence; when Willy returned and discovered his orders had not been carried out, the girl was forthwith chastised with a horsewhip for her ungrateful disobedience. William, it is related, performed the task himself, was promptly arrested, and seems to have avoided prosecution by neglecting to file an insurance claim, according to my informant.

By this time or soon after, the focal point of the huckleberry business on Mary Crose's Mountain—as the upper region of Rock Haven Road was coming to be known—shifted to Mary's own house farther up on the road. The board or tarpaper cabins that had housed berrypickers at the old location were rebuilt in the vicinity of Mary's house. And Mary Crose's

Mary Crose (center), photograph taken in the late 1910s.

kitchen continued to turn out a never-ending supply of food delicious in taste and wondrous in variety. These were the years that truly established Mary's reputation and the pre-eminence of her farm and homestead in the life of the community.

Mary herself was getting on in years. In 1927 her companion, Charles Fisher, died. About 1931 or '32, upon the marriage of her son, Art, Mary retired from her farm and her berrypickers and moved down to a house on the northeast side of the old Minnewaska Trail, just below the lower branch of its triangular junction with Foordmoor Road. This is a large dwelling that was owned at the time by a brother-in-law of Ethel's. Not long afterward, in failing health, Mary moved in with her daughter and son-in-law, Ethel and George Decker, in Kerhonkson. Mary Caston Crose passed away, apparently of cancer, on New Year's Day, 1934.

Mary's retirement and demise did not spell the end of the berrypicking community that bore her name. In fact, the heyday of the huckleberry business on Mary Crose's Mountain occurred during the decade of the 1930s, when Mary Crose's nearly rivaled the entire Smiley Road in output. Starting around the time of Mary's retirement, Wilson and Bertha Addis (the parents of Lawrence Addis) began renting the Mary Crose house during the berry season and expanding the operation to include about forty to sixty cabins and perhaps two hundred pickers. (Addis had bought berries from Mary beginning about 1920; he also bought from the pickers at Sam's Point, but apparently not on the Smiley Road.) Bertha did the measuring and kept a store in the house, where she sold canned food and other supplies to the berrypickers. The couple marketed their huckleberries mostly in Kingston, but shipped some to Newburgh and Albany as well.

Sonny Coddington of Accord, born 1923, picked berries at Mary Crose's from the time he was about six years old. What Sonny remembers best from these years was the lively social life, once the huckleberries were measured and crated and evening began to settle on the mountain. After supper on weekday nights, Sonny recalls, folks would gather around a big campfire to drink and tell stories. Across the road from the main house, Wilson Addis built a dance platform, and on the weekend they'd have a dance, with the music provided by a few of the berrypickers themselves. Summer people from nearby boarding houses or hotels would often come up and join in the fun, the mostly Jewish clientele reportedly mixing comfortably with the local berrypickers.

Wilson and Bertha's grandson Hype Addis, who was born in 1927, has memories of Mary Crose's that predate school age:

> *Grandma used to take me up there in the summertime, and I know I used to go in the back room and dig out the hard sugar, I used to chop it out of the hundred-pound bag to eat it. There was a lot of families up there, a lot of families. Walt Coddington and his family was there, Russ Coddington and his family, they were all there, this man Mr. Ross, he lived alone, he used to ride a bicycle down to Florida every fall, come back in the spring, and they used to call him the Umbrella Man, 'cause he always carried an umbrella with him. And he was always dressed in a little black suit when he went out. There was forty or fifty camps, there was Harry Purcell and his family, eight or ten in his family. Once a week they had a dance, they had a big platform down there, and they had two, three fellas, they had a fiddler and they had a guy who played the squeeze-box and they'd get out there and jig and us kids used to go down there so we could get penny candies. I can remember hanging around the bottom of the platform, my face was about even with the platform. And they drank their beers and hooch, they all had that goin' around.*

The Mr. Ross pictured in the photographs in chapter two is this same "Umbrella Man" referred to above, Hype informs me. At the time of the photos he was spending his summers at the Four-Mile Post. He picked a few berries yet, but was mostly retired.

Another picker at Mary Crose's for many years, a day picker, was a man named Dewitt Carney. He was well known and apparently well liked, and commonly picked over a hundred quarts a day. But quantity was achieved at the expense of quality, and it was rumored that he used a berry rake. "He picked the dirtiest berries on the mountain," I was told.

Wilson and Bertha Addis retired from the huckleberry business about the end of the decade of the thirties. Thereafter, old Dan Decker's son Dan (born 1895) and the latter's wife, Grace (born 1908), took over the job of measuring the berries at Mary Crose's. They turned the harvest over to berry buyer Homer Wynkoop. Dan and Grace lived on Rock Haven Road within a mile or so of the Mary Crose house.

In 1949, some years after the estrangement of Ethel Crose Decker from her husband, George Decker (no identifiable relation to Dan Decker), Ethel and her brother, Art Crose, sold the homestead to Bertha Seibert, who moved into the house with her husband, Frank. The berry business had been in decline, and the last pickers to camp in the cabins there moved out at this time. George Decker purchased land half a mile farther up the mountain and dammed a small swale to form a pond. He built a house by the pond, where he lived summers with his companion, Rae Decker, a daughter of Grace and Dan. Meanwhile, local day pickers continued to bring their huckleberries to Grace and Dan, who resold them to Hype Addis beginning in 1950.

Hype bought berries on the Smiley Road, at Sam's Point, and here on Rock Haven Road, through about 1958. For about the last three years, a shed belonging to George Decker was used for collecting and measuring the huckleberries that Nina Addis and her companions brought down to Decker's from the Four-Mile Post. Rae Decker picked berries herself and also measured the berries picked by Bertha Seibert and a couple of other day pickers, and Hype would buy these as well, before proceeding down the road to buy from Dan and Grace.

Dan Decker passed away in 1959, but Grace continued buying berries till about the early or mid 1960s, reselling them to buyer Paul Gunsch or marketing them directly to area hotels. Through the decade of the sixties, to within a couple of years of her death in 1971, she continued to supply some hotels with berries she picked herself. Her son Irvin also did a small amount of commercial berrypicking, filling orders from friends and neighbors as late as the mid 1970s. Grace and Irvin Decker were the last persons in the huckleberry business on Mary Crose's Mountain.

Once during the summer of 1962, while still in my teens, I hiked up the mountain from the Ukrainian resort on Foordmoor Road to the Four-Mile Post, returning along the path to Decker's house and pond. I was continuing my descent, walking for my first time down Rock Haven Road, when I was pointedly hailed by an old man who emerged from a tiny cabin on the right-hand side of the road, just up from a dwelling of conventional size. He beckoned me inside the shack, placed a bottle of soda pop in my hand (I was sure he'd been quenching his thirst with something more potent), and we spent the next quarter-hour or so in friendly small-talk. Though I don't now recall many specifics of our conversation, I remember gaining the distinct impression that this old-timer would have many interesting stories to tell of his life, if only I'd known where to begin and what to ask so as to create the proper context. When we said goodbye, I noted on my map the location of his cabin and the adjacent house and wrote down the man's name: Frank Seibert.

It was more than two decades later that I dug out my old map and confirmed that this was indeed the former Mary Crose property that Seibert's wife had purchased from Mary's heirs. Bertha Seibert maintained the house, I am told, while Frank usually hung out in what was presumably a former berrypickers' shack, where he drank his wine. My amiable host passed away in December of the same year of our brief encounter.

I have since learned that Frank Seibert was a skilled and highly talented weaver, who made beautiful baskets, bassinets, porch furniture, and such, largely from saplings he cut in the Shawangunk Mountains. He was born 1891 and seems to have first come to the Shawangunk region from New York City about the mid 1930s, when his appearance on the Smiley Road engendered a certain amount of skepticism on the part of Nina Addis and the other folks on the mountain. Hype Addis told me the following story about Frank:

He came up with a crew of men, his wife wasn't with him then, just him and a couple of other people, and they camped on the other side of the Five-Mile Post, and that year no one would sell them anything, 'cause they thought they were revenue men. He had a great big car, a Packard, and his hands were nice and clean, nothing rough about them, and he was dressed up nice. He wasn't a huckleberry picker when he first came in the mountains. The second year he made out all right. He liked to drink from the first time he come here, he was a good drinker. He ended up a wino, but he didn't start out as a wino.

Frank Seibert's quite purposeful solicitation of my company that summer afternoon, not long before his death, almost seems to me, in retrospect, to have revealed him to be a bit prescient. It is surely not uncommon for people in their decline to enjoy a bit of social contact with those whose lives are, in comparison, just beginning—but could he have suspected that his friendly garrulousness would elicit in me just enough sympathetic curiosity to result in my learning and transmitting, many years later, some words about his life and times?

Bertha Seibert sold the old Mary Crose homestead later in 1962; it was purchased by George Decker. Bertha retained lifetime use of the dwelling, and George and Rae continued to live up at the pond summers and down on Foordmoor Road during wintertime. After Bertha's death a few years later, the house was occupied by an old berrypicker named Benny Tripp, who did odd jobs for Decker in exchange for room and board. Benny moved out late in the sixties, George died in 1970, and in subsequent years the house suffered from neglect and worse, so that it long stood uninhabitable and beyond repair. It was demolished in 1992.

George's son Stanley died four years after his father. After many years of poor health, Stanley's mother, Ethel Crose Decker, passed away in 1989, at the age of ninety-five. The site of the homestead is today the property of Diana Decker, who is a daughter of Stanley and thus a great-granddaughter of the matriarch herself.

I have often thought that some enterprising soul, more ambitious than I, might do well to open a good, traditional-style restaurant somewhere nearby and name it Mary Crose's Kitchen. In such a setting proper tribute could perhaps be paid to the woman whose home became a virtual metaphor for culinary hospitality, and whose farm and its surroundings served for half a century as a veritable institution in the economic and social life of the community. Until that day, the surviving place-name, so long as it continues in local usage, will yet demonstrate remembrance of the hard work and good works of this fine woman and the good times enjoyed by so many, on Mary Crose's Mountain.

Chapter 6

Onward
to the Stony Kill

We resume our journey southeastward along the Smiley Road from the trail junction at Polack Swamp and almost immediately note the remains of a rough jeep trail bearing off through the bushes to our right. This trail dates from the 1964 fire; it was not a firebreak, but rather just an access trail for fire fighters, and it leads nowhere in particular. A few minutes later, a similar trail on the left was made by hunters for the purpose of bypassing some troublesome muckholes in the fire road coming up from Decker's.

Just beyond, on the right-hand side, a steep rise of land presents some outcrops alongside the road. From here and from Polack Camp, footpaths led southwestward into the pine barrens where huckleberries grew thickly. These paths found their way to an intermittent rivulet at the bottom of a swale. Though it usually dried up in the heat of the summer, at times Ann's Spring, as it was called, was a place where berrypickers could quench their thirst while out in the field. No one living seems to recall the girl or woman for whom the spring was presumably named. But in June of 1990, Hype Addis agreed to guide me along this branch of the trail to see if the original route could still be followed to its destination (the branch from Polack Swamp having become hopelessly overgrown).

From a single cairn overlooking the road, we bore rightward through the berry bushes; Hype's memory proved its worth as he took me toward the west-southwest, into a broad, shallow depression, then southerly through the lowland, till suddenly there appeared the corner of a rocky ridge of higher ground. Once the climb is made, up out of the thick brush, a row of cairns leads rightward along the edge of the ridge, before curving inland to the left, then following the perimeter of a large, intermittent outcrop. Eventually we turned southeastward, then easterly, to an overlook at the edge of a high plateau. I had already recognized this plateau as a place I'd been to many times before but had always attained via a more easterly approach.

"Ann's Spring" refers to a hole that was dug out somewhere along the watercourse that runs southeastward and lies to the south and southwest of this elevated plateau. Though the spring itself could no longer be precisely located, the route we followed from the Smiley Road rewarded us with the feeling that we indeed were on the original berrypickers' trail of long ago.

Immediately beyond the Ann's Spring trail, the Smiley Road crosses a swale of high-bush berries. The hiker who passes this way in August will scarcely be able to get to the other side without becoming at least a handful or two richer, a sort of reverse-tollbooth procedure. I got much of my own berry harvest here in 1981 and '82. Meinrad (but no one else whom I asked) referred to this as the Bumblebee Swamp, a name also borne by a place near Lake Maratanza.

We reach the highest elevation of the Smiley Road, 1995 feet above the sea. Castle Point dominates the horizon up ahead. As we begin our gradual descent into the upper reaches of the Stony Kill toward the Five-Mile Post, the names of Lou and Ray Quick come to mind, two men whose stories and adventures on the mountain were lived out at both Mary Crose's and the Five-Mile Post, as well as at various locations farther afield. The two were sons of Gus and Jane Quick: Ray was born in December 1900 and Lou in August of 1902, and both lived into their mid eighties. I visited these gentlemen a number of times at their homes in Walden, a few years before their deaths.

Both brothers recalled camping and picking berries at Mary Crose's for a few years during their childhood, sometime about 1910-1917, in the early summer season. The Quick family would then move up to the Five-Mile Post as the berries ripened at higher elevations. Ray boarded with the Croses after the berry season was over one year about 1927, working till springtime with Mary's son, Art, cutting millstones from the Shawangunk conglomerate.

It was at the Five-Mile Post that the Quick brothers did most of their berrypicking. Ray recalled being up there as a child before the age of ten and picking there most summers till about 1945. His record was eighty-six quarts of huckleberries in one day. Lou told me he was at the Five-Mile Post every year from 1910 through 1941, then returned in '48 for a couple of more seasons. Their niece Mazie told me her mother used a huckleberry crate as a bassinet for her when she was an infant.

Lou and Ray's parents had a cabin at the Five-Mile Post just past the main stream crossing, on the right or southwest side of the Smiley Road. Their sons shared a cabin a little farther along the road, on the same side. This according to Hype Addis, who knew them when they were already grown men. But the Slover sisters, who were Lou and Ray's contemporaries at the Five-Mile Post during the first and second decades of the century, remember all the shacks at that time being on the left-hand side of the road.

Both Ray and Lou agree that Frank Barnhart had a store at the Five-Mile Post or ran a store for one Mel Wilkinson. Apparently this closed down during the 1920s. Ray said that Dewey Countryman also had a small store for a time (perhaps the same one that Dewey's father had run during the teens). Nina Addis told me there was never a store at the Five-Mile during the thirties and forties, and that the people came over to the Four-Mile to buy things.

Frank Barnhart and later Bill Countryman measured berries for Paul Gunsch, who was the principal berry buyer. In the mid twenties Gunsch's partner, Jonah Rose, went into business for himself in competition with Gunsch. His daughter married Grover Perkins, who bought berries at the Four-Mile Post. Dewey Countryman—who Lou insisted (and Nina confirmed) was up at the Five-Mile Post well into the 1930s, contrary to Dewey's own memory—measured berries for Jonah Rose. Another early berry buyer at this Smiley Road camp was Melvin Wynkoop, for whom Dewey's father, Mead Countryman, measured berries, according to Lou. Ray Quick didn't remember the Roses or the Slaters ever having a store at the Five-Mile, contrary to what Dewey once told me. Ray did recall having accidentally hit Charles Slater in the head with a stone one time, while playing Duck on the Rock.

During horse and buggy days, said Lou, till about 1920, buyers used to drive in and out via Lakes Minnewaska and Awosting to the east as well as via Ellenville. They were thus able to service some smaller, lesser-known berry camps, until the time when the Smiley family began to encourage a reduction in the squatters' camps and commercial traffic over their vast landholdings. Lou told of a pickers' camp called Long John, halfway between Minnewaska and Awosting, and of another camp in the hardwoods just below the Wolf Jaw (a formation in the southeast face of Margaret's Cliff).

After their berrypicking years were over, the Quick brothers continued to frequent the Shawangunks during deer season. On the forest floor near the head of the Red Spruce Swamp, they built a rude hunters' shanty about 1952. It consisted of a pole frame over which they'd stretch a large, heavy tarp. The tarp was carried back and forth each year on a peculiar single-wheeled conveyance (made from a bicycle wheel), which I discovered years later on the cliff top nearby. Ray and Lou and their hunting companions abandoned this camp after about five years, because of an uncertain water supply and the difficulty of packing things in and out. They camped about two seasons at the stone house ("Seager's Shanty") along the upper Verkeerder Kill, and subsequently built the well-known "Plastic Shack" a little farther upstream.

Lou Quick has seen bears several times in the Shawangunks. The following describes his closest encounter:

> Up above Wolf Jaw I come face to face with one. I thought it was somebody pickin' berries on the other side of the bush, and when I stepped around, there stood the bear. He give a big grunt and he give a jump and he jumped over a log. Where the paw print was on the log was over eight inches. And I guess it give him a pretty good scare, because he give a good big grunt and a jump and away he went, down through there like a fire engine.

Lou Quick worked seventy-two hours straight helping fight the big '39 blaze. He worked under three different fire wardens, local and state. "They each put in for me," Lou recalls, "and so I got paid three times. We were paid twenty-five cents an hour, but I got seventy-five cents. That was pretty good pay at that time, my father was workin' for a dollar a day in the knife shop."

"One night, while we was fightin' the fire down there," says Lou, "I was goin' along the fire line and I seen the biggest bobcat I ever did see, sneakin' along in front of me. I guess he must have weighed forty or fifty pounds. This was near the foot of the mountain, below the New Road. He pretty nearly run in me—passed within about six foot from me, but I don't believe he even saw me. I didn't want to get him in my arms, I wouldn't be able to let loose of him! I jumped back so fast, I knocked the guy down behind me."

Lou suggested I look up Huyler Brasset of Ellenville; I visited Huyler and learned only after his death a few years later that he was a brother of Doris Avery, a former berrypicker whom I'd known for some time. Huyler, born March 1909, told me of summers at the Five-Mile Post from about 1916 through 1924 or '25. Doris confirmed the family's early presence on the mountain but thought it might have begun in 1920, after their mother's marriage to Dan Sheeley. About 1928 Huyler spent a summer at the Four-Mile Post. "There were very few berries that year. Frank 'Doodle' Bradford was there and maybe only a dozen people, because of the bad crop. We'd bring our berries down to Mary Crose's farm."

At the Five-Mile Post Huyler remembered a character named Sam Knapp: "Sam was a regular clown. 'Bout every night when we sat down with a campfire, he always had somethin' to do: He'd go in the camp and out he'd come with a big feather in his hair and a robe around his shoulders and he'd dance an Indian dance around the fire. And then before he got done he'd always dance a rain dance, 'cause he didn't want to pick huckleberries the next day."

We pass the black bear painting that Meinrad made on the cliff face to our right, with the year 1957 chiseled into the rock, and then an overgrown fire trail that heads southwestward toward High Point. This was cut during the 1964 blaze according to Meinrad. But the fire fighters may have simply been clearing out an older fire line, for the official report of the 1947 fire mentions a crew starting work on a line from High Point fire tower northeastward to the Smiley Road. An old trail map in possession of the Mohonk Preserve shows a footpath along this same route, circa 1910.

A minute or two through the woods past the fire trail brings us to the Stony Kill crossing, at the beginning of the Five-Mile Post. The modern route takes us out onto the bedrock at the brink of some small cascades, with a view of Mohonk and a distant vista in clear weather across the Hudson Valley to Massachusetts. The bridge abutments from the original roadway are visible in the bushes to our right. This bridge undoubtedly stood until the 1955 deluge. A bit farther, a short trail leads rightward to the ruins of a cabin of relatively modern construction.

A small, easterly branch of the upper Stony Kill crosses the road a few minutes past the main stream, and shortly before coming to this lesser fork, we arrive at a large flat along the left side of the road where most of the berrypickers' cabins were located. Opposite lies the overturned carcass of a late 1930s automobile, slowly returning to the earth. The flat itself is strewn with artifacts attesting to a once-thriving settlement.

Chapter 7

The Colorful
Countrymen

From its inception until its demise half a century later, the Five-Mile Post was the summertime home, workplace, and playground of the Countryman family. Even as the ravine of the Stony Kill embraced their cabins and campfires during the huckleberry season here on the mountain, the stream's watershed in large part defined the physical realm of this family's existence during the other months as well. For during most of the years of their lives, the Countrymen dwelt never more than a stone's throw from the banks of the Stony Kill or one of its mountain-born tributaries.

Bill Countryman and his sons enjoyed legendary reputations as hard drinkers. But it is also agreed by most that they were well-liked fellows and generally good-humored when not busy fighting amongst themselves. Huyler Brasset told me, "Bill was just like a father to everybody on the mountain. If they had a poor day pickin' huckleberries and didn't have money, he'd buy 'em something to eat." Fred Conklin said the Countryman boys were the same way. Many a time they'd invite young Fred and his brothers to join them for a meal when they were hungry.

Huyler recalled for me one incident in which Bill may have lost his good humor. This occurred about 1922, when Huyler was a boy of thirteen:

*We'd all been out around our campfire at night.
There was a couple of men there, we had a couple of
bottles, and they were drinkin' and havin' a good time.
So finally around ten o'clock we all went to bed. About
an hour later we heard old Bill Countryman hollerin'
and yellin' that a bear was chasin' him. Everybody got
up and run out their camps with flashlights, there's old
Bill with a great big old club, he's poundin' the hell out
of a porcupine. So finally he broke his club and then he
started to run. The porcupine just laid there. The next
morning, we left the old porcupine lay there, and Bill
come out, we told him "Bill, there: You're quite a bear
killer." He didn't talk to any of us for over two weeks.*

Bill was a first-rate millstone cutter and blacksmith in his
younger days. From an early age he had the nickname "Bill
Punch" or "Ol' Bill Punch," though no one I've spoken to
knew the origins of this moniker. Around the campfire at the
Five-Mile Post, he often played the mouth organ and Jew's
harp to entertain family and friends. His son Herman played
accordion and reputedly excelled at the mouth organ. Art
played mouth organ in his youth, and both of the twins were
good tap dancers as children. A long-time friend of the
Countryman family had heard from them a story that Al Jolson
once did a show in Ellenville and saw the twins dance; he
offered to take them on tour with him, but neither the boys nor
their father were apparently interested.

Lawrence Addis told me of something that occurred when
Herman Countryman was a passenger in the former's car, as
they headed from Kerhonkson toward Kingston along Route
209 one day.

As best I recall it, Lawrence's story went something like
this:

*We were approaching a big, slow-moving, open-
bed truck, when Herman told me to move up as close
as possible, he wanted to see what was in the truck. So
then Herman opened the passenger door, he climbed out*

87

onto the running board and onto the fender of the car and jumped in the back of the truck. He rummaged around for something worth taking, but all he found were some apples, so he stuffed his pockets full of them. Then he jumped back onto the car's hood and climbed safely back inside. The driver of the truck never had an idea what was going on.

Lou Quick described an instance in which Oscar Countryman displayed a daring comparable to that shown by his older brother: This occurred about the 1930s as Oscar was riding up the mountain with Paul Gunsch. At the Three-Mile Post they spotted a rattlesnake on or near the road. Oscar jumped out of the truck and stomped it to death, though he was wearing only sneakers on his feet at the time.

The following story was told to me by Rae Decker, who said this occurred about 1948, when she was living with George Decker along old Route 44/55 above Kerhonkson. At the time, Bill Countryman and his sons lived on the lower end of the old New Paltz-Wawarsing Turnpike, about 150 yards up the hill from where it joins Upper Granite Road:

Oscar and Art came down the road that day and stopped at Rae and George's house with two brand-new white shirts to sell. The goods were in their original packaging. "We were butchering pigs that day," Rae recalls. George gave the twins two dollars for the shirts. Old Bill came down a day or two later and made inquiry. Bill explained that he'd hidden these shirts away so in case something should happen to him, at least he'd have something decent to be buried in! "They'd sell the boots right off their feet" when they needed money for a bottle, according to Rae.

Bill had told Rae and George that if ever his sons should come along with something to sell, "Buy it from them; at least that way I'll know where to find it."

Rae remembered hearing from George of another occasion, when Bill and his three sons were up at the Five-Mile Post drinking, and Bill fell smack into a tub full of laundry that was

ABBREVIATED GENEALOGY: ROSE/COUNTRYMAN; ROSE/QUICK/ADDIS

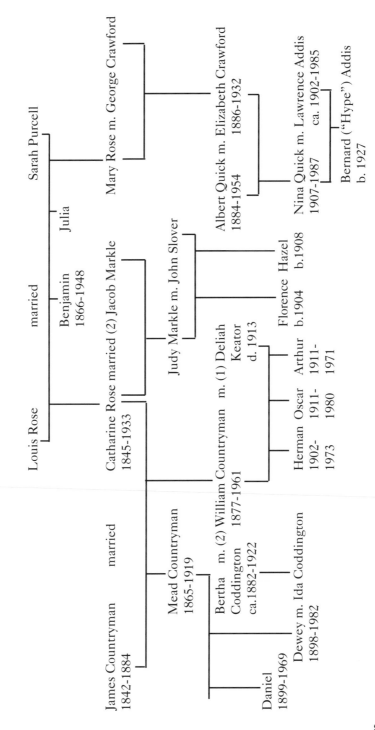

soaking. The bottle flew out of his grasp and went crashing on the rocks. The boys then went down on all fours and managed to save some of the precious liquid by putting spoons, or even their lips, to the hollows and cracks in the rock. This story I heard from a few sources. Reportedly, as Bill sat there in the tub of laundry, he exclaimed, "Rubbedy-dub-dub, Bill Punch in the tub!"

Bill Countryman was born June 22, 1877, to James and Catharine Jane (Rose) Countryman. Bill had an older brother, Mead, whose son Dewey I met back in 1980. Bill also had a younger brother, named Jason. The boys' father died when Bill was seven years old. Shortly thereafter their mother married Jacob Markle. Catharine had three children from this second marriage.

In 1865 James Countryman had purchased fifty acres of land running from the New Paltz-Wawarsing Turnpike southward beyond the Sanders Kill. This was a long, narrow tract comprising a portion of the western half of great lot number twelve of the Groot Transport of the Rochester Patent. The land was apparently left to his widow upon his death. The upper part of this property is still known as Caddie's Big Hill, and contained a hollow that was said to mark the foundation of the dwelling of Catharine and James Countryman.

Six-tenths of a mile north along modern Route 44/55 from where the highway crosses the Sanders Kill, a lane crosses the highway and leads southwestward eight or ten minutes by foot to a millstone quarry on the property. The old foundation was at a higher elevation somewhere nearby, to the left of the lane or quarry as one ascends. It is possible that Bill and his brothers were born here and that the millstone quarry was a source of income for James Countryman as well as the place where young Bill first learned the craft.

At some point after her first husband's death, Catharine took on two partners in joint ownership of this land: her son Jason and Mary Elizabeth Markle, Catharine's stepdaughter from a previous marriage of Jacob Markle. In August of 1902, this land was purchased from the three by Bill Countryman.

The former Countryman homestead on the New Paltz-Wawarsing Turnpike, ca. 1930. The cloud of smoke is from blasting during construction of Route 44/55.

Prior to this, Bill had married Deliah Keator, who is said to have been part Indian. Their oldest child was a girl named Lewella. There was also a daughter Eva. Herman was born in 1902 and the fraternal twins, Arthur and Oscar, in 1911. Another son, Fred, described to me by a contemporary as an extremely likeable boy, was a year older than Herman but died at the tender age of fifteen, a victim of typhoid. Deliah died in childbirth in early April 1913, a doctor having reportedly warned at the time the twins were born that she could not survive another birth.

During these years, Bill and his young family lived on the lower end of the tract purchased from his mother, in a small, old frame house on the New Paltz-Wawarsing Turnpike. Seven-tenths of a mile up the Turnpike from its junction with the Upper Granite Road, on the right-hand side, the cellar foundation of the Countryman home is still clearly visible. This, and not the site higher up on Caddie's Big Hill, may in fact have been Bill's birthplace or perhaps his childhood home for all but the earliest years. The site was shown to me by Miss

Nellie May Van Wagner, a tough and independent lady who, despite her diminutive size and considerable age, was keeping her house warm with wood she'd cut up herself with a gasoline-powered chain saw. Nellie May was born February 1915 in this same house, which stands across the road and just a bit uphill from the site of the former Countryman home.

Nellie May's parents were Silas and Lottie (Rose) Van Wagner. Silas's sister was Mary (Van Wagner) Quick, who camped at the Four-Mile Post, by the trail junction. Lottie's father was John Rose, and John's father was Lewis Rose, who may have been a cousin to the man by the same name who was an ancestor of the Addis and Countryman families. Both Nellie May and the late Nina Addis spoke of being distant cousins to one another through the Rose family. John Rose and his son (Nellie May's uncle) William made barrel hoops in the main part of the house before Nellie May was born: Metal blades on a wooden contraption operated with a foot pedal shaved saplings into the flat bands used for barrel hoops. These were in great demand during the canal days of the nineteenth century. "I'm a hoopy, I was born in a hoop shop," Nellie May told me with a grin.

There were many day pickers who would walk, ride, or drive past the house on their way up the road, returning loaded down with huckleberries, which they'd bring to Lottie and her daughter, who measured the berries for a number of different buyers over the years. Nellie May told me she and her mother used to handle four or five crates a day during the season. She herself picked huckleberries from childhood and continued measuring for outside berry buyers until the mid 1950s.

Bill Countryman sold the entire fifty-acre parcel in May of 1914. Nellie May always understood that the sale was necessitated by a large, unpaid grocery debt that had been accumulating at a local store. Within a year or two of his wife's death, about the time he parted company with his house and land, Bill took a common-law wife, a rather scrawny woman who went by the name of Cricket. They lived in a house belonging to Bill's half-sister Judy (Markle) Slover and her husband, John Slover, on Stony Kill Road. In later years Nina Addis's house was built on the foundation where this house had stood. About 1918 Bill married Bertha Coddington. There were two daughters from this marriage.

I believe Bill and Bertha lived somewhere on Stony Kill Road at first and then moved back up on the Turnpike as tenants in the old Countryman homestead; Nellie May is certain she remembers the Countrymen living there during her early childhood, and another informant also remembers hearing that Bill had lived here with Bertha. Sometime about 1920 they moved back down to the valley, where Bertha died in 1922, at the age of forty. Bertha's daughter from a prior marriage married Bill's nephew Dewey Countryman.

I have been told that Bill treated his women and children harshly and that he'd sometimes come home drunk with friends, wake up the boys, and make them dance a jig while he played music, for the entertainment of his guests. There is also a story Nellie May told me that his first wife's death supposedly occurred after Bill had picked her up, carried her outdoors, and plunged her into a tub of cold water, out of anger or to induce labor—this in early springtime. But in later years, by most accounts, Bill seems to have mellowed considerably.

Bill's mother, Catharine ("Caddie"), twice widowed, lived down on the Stony Kill Road a mile and four and one-half tenths northeast of the junction with Upper Granite Road, on the right-hand side as you travel toward Accord. Her house still stands but has been enlarged and its original appearance altered beyond recognition. I suspect the property came to Caddie through her second husband, Jacob Markle, though I've been unable to establish this for certain. In 1913 Catharine sold this property to her son Oscar Markle (also spelled "Maracle"). But Catharine continued residing here, apparently alone and independent, until her death in 1933 at the age of eighty-eight. Nellie May Van Wagner told me a story about Catharine that was later confirmed for me by the latter's granddaughter Florence (Slover) Pitkin: that Caddie was known to keep her money secreted somewhere in the field out back of her house

Catharine Markle at her home on Stony Kill
Road. Photo believed taken in the 1910s.

on Stony Kill Road, in a small purse "hidden under a dry old
cow flop."

From about 1920 until his mother's death, Bill Countryman
and his children lived in the Granite area, residing during most
or all of these years somewhere on Stony Kill Road, southwest
of his mother's house. Upon Catharine's passing, Bill moved
into the house that now belonged to his half-brother Oscar. The
latter died intestate in 1942, and the property went to his
widow, Elsie, and their son Earl. When Elsie died in 1945, Earl
sold the property to Francis Hasbrouck. Bill Countryman
continued to live here in his mother's old house at least until
then, and probably for another year or two.

Herman Countryman married in 1926 and brought his teenage wife into his father's household on Stony Kill Road. With Bertha gone, Luella took care of her young half-sisters. Herman worked with his father at stone cutting. Later on, the boys generally took employment where they could find it, as laborers and handymen. Herman's marriage lasted several years. After his wife's departure, he resided at various places in and around Ulster County. He was with Gertrude Bennet for some years; his union with May Skiff began in the 1940s, lasting into the early or middle 1960s. During much of their time together, May joined Herman and the latter's brothers on the mountain during huckleberry season.

At the age of seventeen or eighteen, Art married a girl named Ethel Robinson. The union lasted just long enough for his wife to give birth to three daughters (two of whom Art acknowledged as his own). They lived in New Paltz together, where the first of their children was born in March of 1930. Upon dissolution of the marriage, Art reportedly lost contact permanently with his children and former wife.

He and Oscar continued to live on and off with their father until their departure for wartime service in 1942. In a military hospital, Oscar met a woman named Evelyn Brazelton who was working as a nurse's aide. Although they never chose to marry, Evelyn lived with Oscar for over twenty years and informally took the Countryman name. Art had a girlfriend named Caroline with whom he maintained an intermittent relationship. She joined the family during summertime on the mountain for a couple of years beginning about the end of the 1940s.

After the War, Bill, Art, Oscar, and Evelyn moved together from Caddie's old place on the Stony Kill Road onto the New Paltz-Wawarsing Turnpike, not to the family's old home but to a small cottage much lower down, on the same side of the road, immediately above the spot now occupied by a modern brick house. They lived here rent-free in exchange for doing woodcutting, carpentry, and miscellaneous labor for Rodney Smith, who owned the property and lived in an adjacent house.

Smith trucked firewood down to New York City, also loads of sawdust for butcher shops, and returned with apple boxes and various sorts of storage crates, which he'd sell to area farmers. Bill sometimes accompanied him on these trips to help with loading and unloading.

This is where they were living when the incident with the two shirts occurred, related earlier. Rae Decker tells another story from this period, one that occurred at night when she and George were driving down the old Turnpike. As they approached the bottom of the hill, where the Turnpike meets Upper Granite Road, they saw two figures in the middle of the road that they supposed were "two dogs, a male and female, stuck fast." George brought the car to a halt, and in the headlights they recognized Evelyn and Oscar, with a bottle between them, getting to their feet and shuffling slowly over to the side of the road. The Deckers didn't address them then and never subsequently told the two about their original notion, but Rae did relate it to a gathering of friends and drew quite a howl of laughter! It was Nellie May Van Wagner who originally alerted me to the story.

Bill Countryman's last summer at the Five-Mile Post was probably 1949. He shared a cabin with Art and Caroline, while Herman camped with May Skiff and two of her children, Alice and Ed. These cabins were on the left side of the road. Bill spent the summer of 1950 camping at Sam's Point, where he measured berries for Paul Gunsch, as he had done at the Five-Mile Post. In 1951 he was absent from Sam's Point, but returned for the summers of 1952 and '53 before finally retiring from the life of the huckleberry camps.

During the decade of the forties, the population of the Five-Mile Post dwindled to a remnant. According to the recollections of Fred and Alice Conklin and Fred's younger brother Danny, even the Countryman brothers spent the better part of each summer at the Four-Mile Post, at least since the end of the War, moving over to the Five only for the swampberry season in mid August. Other folks picked swampberries in this vicinity on August days, but returned to

Oscar and Evelyn, August 1961.

their cabins at the Four-Mile Post in the evening. Hype Addis remembers Art and Caroline and Herman and May and the latter's children being the only pickers still camping at the Five-Mile Post when he bought berries here in August of 1950. That was Hype's first year as a berry buyer, and he managed to squeeze out Paul Gunsch by offering a better price to the handful of people still camping here. It was the final summer that any berrypickers camped at the Five-Mile Post; by 1951, the last of the old camps on the upper Stony Kill lay abandoned.

In the fall of 1956, Art moved out of the family household and began boarding with Lillian (Crawford) Wood in Summitville, southwest along the valley from Ellenville. About three years later, Bill, Oscar, and Evelyn also moved down off the Turnpike, to a cottage on Upper Granite Road, which they rented from a Mr. Katz. They stayed here only a short while before moving nearby into a cabin owned by Lawrence Addis. This was one of a cluster of cabins on the south side of the Stony Kill, immediately west of the junction of Upper Granite

Road with the Stony Kill Road. The Countryman cabin was the last one in back, on the bank of the kill. It subsequently burned or was torn down.

This was the last home of Bill Countryman. About 1960, walking home drunk one night from Kerhonkson, he fell off the Stony Kill bridge and suffered a broken leg. He was cared for in the County Home outside of New Paltz and returned home after some months. He got around on crutches for a year or so before a mild heart attack sent him to the hospital in Kingston. He died during his convalescence at a Kingston nursing home August 13, 1961, at the age of eighty-four.

About 1967, Herman, having broken up with May Skiff, moved in with Fred and Alice (Skiff) Conklin and their family on Clinton Avenue in Ellenville, followed about 1968 by Oscar, whom Evelyn had left a year or two before. They were joined in the spring of 1970 by their brother Art, after his friend Lillian no longer had the patience to deal with his drunkenness. While living in Summitville, Art had walked into a tree and hit his head badly, Lillian told me. He always complained of headaches after that. In December of 1971, while living on Clinton Avenue, he reportedly took a bad fall, suffering a head injury that may have been exacerbated by an argument ending in fisticuffs. He died of a brain hemorrhage. But the coroner told Lillian there was evidence of a brain tumor as well.

Herman died in January 1973, apparently of acute alcoholism. After a tragic fire the next year in which two of the Conklin children perished, Fred and his remaining family moved to a cottage on Berme Road. Oscar lived there in a tiny adjacent cabin until 1980, when, like his older brother before him, he died of an apparent alcohol overdose.

After Evelyn left Oscar, she continued to reside in and about the Granite, Kerhonkson, and Accord neighborhood. She had been a free-wheeling character in her days with Oscar and his family and something of a notorious personality both on and off the mountain. But in her old age she is said to have become very respectable and straight-laced. Her eyesight failing, she passed away in 1985 at the age of seventy-four.

Behind a white picket fence along the southeast side of Stony Kill Road, seven-tenths of a mile from its junction with Upper Granite Road, a small, rural cemetery bears the remains of the Countryman clan. Bill, Herman, Oscar, and Art are there, as is Bill's mother, Catharine Markle, his brother Mead, the latter's sons Dewey and Daniel, and Catharine's brother Benjamin Rose, with his wife and some of their children. Evelyn lies buried there too.

So Bill Countryman and his boys are united once again. And whether their lives are viewed as alcoholic tragedy or rustic comedy, it can not be denied that a vigorous spirit of camaraderie infused their collective existence. Of the folks who knew them, a few found little to praise, but most found them good-hearted and generous, sociable and genuinely likeable. Bill's reputed behavior toward his women and his own young children is surely indefensible. But otherwise, most of the negative impulses of father and sons were directed strictly toward themselves and one another, in a fatalistic, love-hate relationship exemplified by an instance related to me by Herman's ex-wife, when Bill and his sons became involved in a drunken brawl with each other that ended in their falling into an alcoholic sleep, still locked in each other's embraces.

During their most boisterous period together, Bill and the twins shared the company of the one woman who appears to have been their equal in every respect, and who may have helped to hold their lives together even as she shared in, and at times exceeded, their own excesses. Bill departed this world at a ripe old age, seemingly with his chin up. But with their father gone, with Evelyn and May's departure, and with the failure of Art's attempt at a stable life in Summitville, the three sons began returning one by one for their final, sad reunion, mourners filing in wearily for their own funerals, which they awaited and proceeded to expedite with drinks in hand.

Down in the valley of the lower Stony Kill, the Countrymen lie in peace at last with themselves and each other. But here at the Five-Mile Post, in the upper reaches of the same stream, where valley and mountaintop are nearly one,

Bill Countryman and his three sons will always be very much alive: roaming the woods and the rocky slabs for huckleberries, making music and jigging around the evening campfire, laughing, fighting, and of course drinking, far into the Shawangunk night.

Chapter 8

The Five-Mile Post
to Lake Awosting

Nina Addis once told me her parents had bought a cabin here at the Five-Mile Post from an old man named Paul Lange. I later questioned Nina about this and she affirmed that it was unusual for anyone to pay money for a cabin, the berrypickers having been squatters who possessed title to neither land nor buildings along the Smiley right-of-way. More commonly a family or individual either built a shanty or simply appropriated and repaired one that had been abandoned. But Nina's folks were friends of the man, and when he was ready to retire from camping up there, they were evidently willing to make payment so as to be sure of reserving for their own use what may have been a better than average structure.

Long before Nina's time, this Paul Lange had been the subject of a poem appearing on pages eighty through eighty-three of an 1891 book of poetry entitled *Songs of the Shawangunks*. The author, Ralcy H. Bell of Rosendale, wrote that Lange came over from Germany somewhere about 1860 and had a cabin in the northern Shawangunks. This would not likely have been the cabin at the Five-Mile Post that Nina spoke of, for in 1891 the Smiley Road did not yet exist, and the text of the poem indicates Lange lived in his cabin year-round with his wife and child, suggesting a location somewhat more accessible to the valley.

And here among the Shawangunks blue
he met and loved his wife:
A dark-eyed, winsome woman, true,
A jewel in his life.
And here among the mountains wild
He built his humble home,
And dwelleth here with wife and child,
Nor careth he to roam.

In light of these romantic lines, it is interesting to note what Nina related to me regarding Paul Lange's later years:

He used to call me "Kitten." And when he was selling his camp to my mother and father, he was through with the old mountains, 'cause he was quite an old man then, and I know he had a big moustache and whatnot, and his sons, at that time, and his wife, used to live down on this Stony Kill Road. But he himself kept more to himself. When he got through camping there, then he came down, off the mountain, with his family, and later on in years, he built himself an old camp up by the Slupp Brook. And that's where he lived. His family lived in the house and he lived in this old camp.

A tributary of the Stony Kill runs parallel to the Stony Kill Road, on the road's southeast side; the Slupp Brook, as I have learned, is a smaller tributary that comes down off the mountain and enters the larger one a mile due south of the hamlet of Accord.

Perhaps Paul Lange careth not to roam, but we still have a long way to walk, and the Smiley Road beckoneth. Before leaving this spot, however, the Five-Mile Post has more of its history to reveal to us. For this we are indebted to Florence Pitkin (born June 1904) and Hazel Kaup (born May 1908), sisters who spent their childhood here at the Five-Mile Post during the early years of its existence as a settlement. They summered here from birth through 1915, living during the remainder of the year down in the valley in a house on whose foundation Nina Addis's house was later built. Their parents were John Slover and Judith (Markle) Slover; Judith was a daughter of Catharine (nee Rose) through the latter's marriage to Jacob Markle, after the death of her first husband, James Countryman. Florence and Hazel were thus half-first cousins to Herman, Art, and Oscar Countryman, and Bill Countryman was the sisters' half-uncle.

The Slover family moved to another house about 1913 and then to Walden in 1915, where the two sisters still reside as of this writing. Two years later there was a widespread polio outbreak, so the family went back up to the Five-Mile Post for one last summer, for the protection of their young daughters. And in fact, none of the children at the huckleberry camp contracted the dread disease, though some of Florence and Hazel's classmates who'd stayed in Walden were not so lucky.

Florence told me she recalled there being about a hundred people at the Five-Mile Post during her typical childhood summer. Her family came and went by way of Minnewaska, not Ellenville, so the sisters never once visited the Four-Mile Post or other berry camps down the Smiley Road. Both Florence and Hazel recall playing Duck on the Rock with the other children; they remember the Slater brothers, Tracy and Charles; and they were childhood companions and lifelong friends of Lou and Ray Quick. Florence and Hazel remember their maternal grandmother, Catharine, at the Five-Mile Post. "She used to go barefoot pickin' berries," they told me, "she was a toughy!" Caddie's sister Julia was there, with her husband, George Conklin, and their sons Ben, George, Alonzo, John, and Pete. And they remember Caddie and Julia's brother Benny Rose, with his wife, Carrie (Markle), "a little bit of a woman," and their many sons and daughters: Lew, Art, Russel, Ed, Mamie (Mary), Alice, Neddy, Lucy, Laurie, Ethel, and Amy. These children and the Conklin brothers were all first cousins to Florence and Hazel's mother.

The two sisters remembered well something Nina Addis had described to me, the horse-drawn surrey that passed by along the Smiley Road in those days, carrying guests of the Lake Minnewaska Mountain Houses to and from the Ellenville railway station: "Us kids knew when they was coming, we'd all gang out along the road, and then they'd throw candy or pennies to us. That was a big deal! They were some real stylish ladies." They shared with me as well some other recollections of life at the Five-Mile Post: "It was a must that you all have new sunbonnets to wear at the beginning of the season," they told me. The women and girls would sew them during the preceding winter or spring and show them off as they arrived at the berry camp. The bonnets helped shield their faces from the sun's rays during the long summer days of berrypicking. The men and boys generally wore wide-brimmed hats for the same reason.

"There used to be men who would bring these big black bears up there, I imagine maybe from a circus or something down in Ellenville," recall the two sisters. The bears would walk up the mountain either chained to the back of a wagon or simply held on a chain by the trainers, who would make a few dollars by stopping with the animals wherever there were berrypickers camped. The first time they ever encountered this act, Florence and Hazel were sitting on the rocks along the edge of the road, a couple of minutes northwest of the camp:

> *There we sat on those rocks. And I looked around the turn, and I see these bears coming up. I didn't know yet there was men with them. Hazel was small, I grabbed hold of her and I ran with her all the way to the camp! They'd get 'em up a tree, and these bears'd do stunts up in the tree, and then these guys'd pass a hat around and say, "The bears won't come down unless you pay." So my father said, "Well lookit, we don't give a damn whether they come down or not!"*

Fred Conklin remembered his paternal grandmother telling of the stunt bears making their appearance over at the Three-Mile Post:

My grandmother Alice Conklin used to say she could remember when this guy would come up with this black bear, with a chain and a collar on him. And he'd make wagers with anybody if they could wrassle the bear down. But nobody ever beat the black bear. The bear could do tricks besides his wrestle. There was people scoured up with the bear, pretty good at times. Somebody would be drinkin' and stuff and they thought they could take the bear on, and they would get scoured up on the rocks. This is the stories have been told to me, this was before my time.

Up on Sam's Point, Lillian Wood had a vague memory from childhood of a visit by a trained bear. This would be about the mid to late 1920s. She told me the bear was so tame she fed it peanuts. "It ate right out of my hand. I guess that's why I've always loved bears."

Somewhere back perhaps a couple of hundred yards south or southwest of the Smiley Road, there may once have stood a hoop cutter's cabin or even hoop-shaving shed belonging to Ace Whitaker, at a time long before the Smiley Road was built. Nina Addis told me that when she was a young girl, at the Five-Mile Post with her family, she remembers having seen here the actual remains of "Ace's Shanty" (as the place was called)—though she may have been confused about this recollection, for Florence and Hazel, who were her contemporaries, are sure nothing remained of the shanty itself. Hype Addis told me that a well-worn footpath left the Smiley Road just beyond the more easterly branch of the Stony Kill and led upstream to some good swampberries, at the place that everyone referred to as "Ace's Shanty." Hype's knowledge of the place-name derives from Herman Countryman, who took him picking there in the 1930s. Florence and Hazel remember it as the ridge of exposed rock extending southwestward from the Five-Mile Post, *between* the two branches of the kill: People always spoke of picking berries "up *on* Ace's Shanty," they told me, never "down in" or even "up in."

Proceeding eastward, the Smiley Road runs for three-quarters of a mile at a level grade, through an area of woodsy shade. There is scarcely a single landmark or distinguishing natural feature along this stretch until one comes to a rock outcrop that crosses the road and around which the latter makes a rightward bend. A large pine tree to the right of the road, at the near edge of the outcrop, helps to make this a pleasant spot, a sort of aesthetic resting place from the physiographic monotony that precedes it. The first time ever I passed this way (headed westward, as it happens), I jotted down on my map the name Pine Rest and noted that it would make a nice stopping place for lunch someday. Though I've passed here many a time since, I have yet to do so at a time of day suitable for a meal; which has been a source of very slight but persistent frustration to me.

Another source of frustration is that this is yet another place that some have identified as "Ace's Shanty." Specifically, Ray Quick said it was in the woods just to the south of this rock outcrop. His brother Lou located the place-name "between the Five-Mile Post and the Fly Brook," which more nearly conforms to this location than to the other. And Huyler Brasset told me Ace's Shanty was on the south side of the Smiley Road, shortly before the descent toward the Fly Brook, a description that corresponds comfortably to this spot. These three men were all contemporaries of Nina, Florence, Hazel, and Herman. (Lou Quick is my only oral source for the name Ace Whitaker.) Hype Addis told me he remembers a shanty here as recently as the 1940s, but that it most assuredly was not Ace's Shanty. He thinks it might have been the berrypicking cabin of Frank Seibert.

Asaph D. Whitaker, as I've since learned from archival sources, lived 1815-1868 and owned many hundreds of acres in the Shawangunk Mountains, including the whole of great lot twenty of the Groot Transport and most of lot nineteen. Lot twenty stretches southeastward from the cliff line below Napanoch Point and includes the site of the Five-Mile Post and the first Ace's Shanty; Whitaker's holdings in lot nineteen included the site of the second Ace's Shanty, nearer to the Fly Brook. At the time of his death, Whitaker resided in Kerhonkson. His obituary in *The Ellenville Journal* of August 1, 1868 notes that "Col. Asaph D. Whitaker" had been "for many years one of the most esteemed and influential citizens of this town," a description that suggests a wealthy, politically connected businessman rather more than a mountain rustic.

Perhaps Ace Whitaker had a cabin in each of the two places, either contemporaneously or consecutively. Then again, perhaps he was only the landlord. Regardless of where the actual cabin(s) may have stood, as a place-name "Ace's Shanty" seems destined to remain ambiguous.

Before long the road bears to the left and drops in altitude, soon bringing us to the old bridge abutments on the Fly Brook, which here is a lovely, sunlit stream flowing gently over smooth bedrock. The modern route of the Smiley Road turns a sharp right, descends the embankment, and fords the brook just below the site of the old bridge. I'm almost certain Blacky had told me back in 1962 that there was once a Six-Mile Post here, and Dewey Countryman affirmed that in the second decade of the century there were a small number of tents and pickers at the Fly Brook crossing. But Lou Quick was adamant that there was never a camp at this location, Florence (Slover) Pitkin didn't remember one, and Hype Addis never heard of a camp here; though it seems an attractive site, with abundant water, it may be presumed that any settlement that may have been here was relatively small and very short-lived.

From this location an old carriage road, which may easily be mistaken for the continuation of the Smiley Road itself, begins its mile-and-a-half descent to the Stony Kill, far below. In days gone by the road crossed the Stony Kill and continued down the mountain to connect with Rock Haven Road. The lower portion, at least, was known as the Whittaker or High Point Road. I was told by Lou Quick that coal from Kerhonkson used to be hauled up the mountain by horse and buggy along this route to the summer camp at Lake Awosting, in the early years of the century.

Ray Quick related that old Dan Decker, who married Mary Crose's sister Ella, was found to be poaching timber or hoop saplings on Smiley property this side of the Stony Kill, and that the Smileys put an end to the problem by removing enough of the bridge to prevent vehicular access from below. Hype Addis remembers that, when he was a boy in the 1930s, there were yet a few log beams across the kill here. The old through-route may yet be traced in the form of a footpath that leads northeastward, beginning a little downstream and across the kill from the spot where the present carriage road terminates. A few minutes below the site of the old bridge is Stony Kill Falls, where the water drops some ninety or ninety-five feet. A cousin of Ben Conklin and Bill Countryman named Daisy Booth reportedly fell to her death here at the age of about fourteen.

The Smiley Road bridge across the Fly Brook, like the Stony Kill bridge far below, was taken away (or rather, incapacitated) by the Smiley family, who removed the cross-planks from the log beams and piled them up on the southeast side of the brook. Their concern in this case was to prevent huckleberry traffic from infringing upon the privacy and quiet of the Minnewaska resort lands. For this information I am indebted to Hype Addis, who told me of one occasion in the early forties when the old Fly Brook bridge was called to duty for one last vehicular crossing:

> *There was Alfred Calvin, and Frankie Quick, and myself: us three, we were supposed to go pickin' huckleberries, we was about fifteen years old. We went over there with Mother's old '29 Buick, we decided we'd carry the plank all across and put it back on the bridge, just to see if we could do it. It took us two or three hours, we drove the Buick across the bridge, and when we got across the bridge there was a low-hangin' limb, we run into that, it knocked the windshield off the old Buick. As we come back across the bridge the timbers kept making a snappin' sound. But they didn't break. So we drove back home to the Four-Mile Post,*

as we drove up I shoved my hand through the broken windshield and waved at Mother. What else could I do?

"Did you get. . ."

"Yes I did," Hype laughed, without waiting for me to finish the question.

A few minutes after crossing the Fly Brook, our route veers leftward and climbs steeply. Finally we reach the end of our journey at Awosting Lake, the eastern terminus of the Smiley Road. The original route from here to Minnewaska now goes by the name of Upper Awosting Trail: It crosses Huntington Ravine, skirts Litchfield Ledge, and traverses the long ridge above the Peters Kill, arriving at the northwest corner of Lake Minnewaska near the site of Wildmere, the larger of the two Minnewaska Mountain Houses.

But we will set our sights in precisely the opposite direction: If we follow the carriage road for a short distance clockwise around the lake, we'll arrive at a high overlook with a spectacular view southwestward, across the far end of Awosting. Four miles distant is the flatish dome of Sam's Point, where more huckleberry history awaits telling.

Part II

Lillian Wood and Sam's Point

Chapter 9

Origins
and Early Years

It is probably fair to assume that throughout the Shawangunk region, people began making day trips to pick huckleberries for family consumption as early as the 1700s, and that a small amount of local commerce in berries gradually evolved with the improvement of wagon roads and increase in population. *The Ellenville Journal*, on microfilm at the Ellenville Public Library, provides our first documentary references to the berry business, under a column variously entitled "Home Record," "Home Matters," and "Local Notes":

Under date of July 18, 1862 we find a report that "Whortleberries have begun to find their way into our market, although for some reason or another the crop hereabouts this season is not nearly as abundant as usual." The word *huckleberry* thereafter replaces the earlier form, appearing sometimes in quotations; there is mention made on July 23, 1864 and both July 18 and August 1, 1868. On the latter date, the *Journal* reports, "—The huckleberry buyers have been paying only eight cents per quart for some days past." These early references would seem to describe an industry in which day pickers supplied predominantly local markets, through the agency of buyers (wholesalers/distributors).

On the mountain's northwest slope, the full establishment of resident berrypicking communities may be closely linked to the opening of the Smiley Road in 1901. But just how long ago did pickers begin to build their squatters' cabins at Sam's Point and to camp there in significant numbers? The plank road from Ellenville across the mountain to Newburgh and the first good road to Sam's Point from Cragsmoor were both constructed in the 1850s, and it seems unlikely that a Sam's Point community serviced by outside berry buyers could have existed prior to then. (*The Ellenville Journal* of July 13, 1849 describes in great detail an excursion on foot to Sam's Point the previous August tenth, but though it speaks of "a plain of large extent, nearly level, thinly covered with stunted shrub-oaks and dwarf pines," there is no mention in the lengthy article of any fires, shacks, berrypickers, or even berry bushes.)

The extension of the rail line north to Ellenville in 1871 was apparently an important factor in the growth of the huckleberry business. As early as July 1, 1871, *The Ellenville Journal* reports that

> —*The "huckleberry" season has opened, and pickers have been several days engaged on the mountain. L. Meinhold and others are buying at booths near the foot of the mountain, and thousands of bushels of Shawangunk berries, the finest in the world, will during the next few weeks find their way to New York. From this vicinity the berries will be shipped mainly by rail. At present the pickers receive fifteen cents per quart.*

Although most of this crop was harvested by day pickers in the pre-Smiley Road era, perhaps the settlement at Sam's Point dates from that decade. Writing in 1883 in the *Bulletin of the Torrey Botanical Club*, N.L. Britton refers to "great quantities of *Vaccinium Pennsylvanicum*" (low-bush blueberry) both above and below the cliff at Sam's Point, and to "an abundant growth of *Pinus rigida* (pitch pine) above the cliff, "very much stunted in growth. . . and forming low, straggling bushes, few of them more than five feet high. . . ." This description strongly suggests the presence of berrypickers' fires at Sam's Point by that year.

From a collection of glass plate negatives of local scenes, Ellenville area, ca. 1902-1907. Note the berry box worn by the fellow on left. (Courtesy of Phil Aaron, Ellenville, New York.)

Much of what I have learned about berrypicking at Sam's Point during the present century comes from Lillian Wood, a remarkable woman with a tenacious spirit and strong sense of history. Although Lillian herself played a modest supporting role in the quiet drama of Shawangunk berrypicking, her life intersected in divers ways with the lives of many of its principal players. It was the genealogical clues and information she provided that helped reveal to me the familial relationships linking so many of the personalities prominent in the mountain's history. Lillian herself occupies a branch on this extended family tree.

Lillian was born May 27, 1923, in the hamlet of Ulsterville, township of Shawangunk, in the large, old frame building that was long known as White's Tavern (now Cronin's). Her father was Ben Crawford (1898-1962), who measured berries on Sam's Point for Hype Addis during the 1950s. Lillian told me her father's father, William D. Crawford, was a farmer. "He sold his vegetables, he had at one time probably about two hundred chickens when I was a little girl, he had a milkin' cow, he had a team of horses, and as years went on, he got a goat." The Crawford land lay along the east side of Cox Road on the slope of Shawangunk Mountain, near the hamlet of Pleasant Valley in Mamakating township. Ben Crawford was one of nine children, all born in a log cabin according to Lillian, who told me she has cousins yet living on portions of the ancestral land.[1]

Lillian's mother, Julia (1906-1940), was the daughter of Maude Donnelly (also spelled Donely), who first married Bill Hamilton and later Ben Conklin. I've written about Ben in connection with the Smiley Road berry camps. Although conceived during the first marriage, Lillian's mother was born after the second and bore the Conklin surname. Maude left Ben Conklin after a couple of years and went back with Bill

---

[1] At some point in his life, Lillian's grandfather had evidently reversed the order of his first and middle names, for he was born February 4, 1863 with the name Daniel W. Crawford. His father, also named Daniel, was a Union soldier (Fifteenth New York Artillery) who died of disease in 1864, the same year he'd entered the service. Lillian recalls a framed photograph of her great-grandfather, in military uniform, hanging in her grandfather's house.

ABBREVIATED GENEALOGY: ROSE/CONKLIN/CRAWFORD

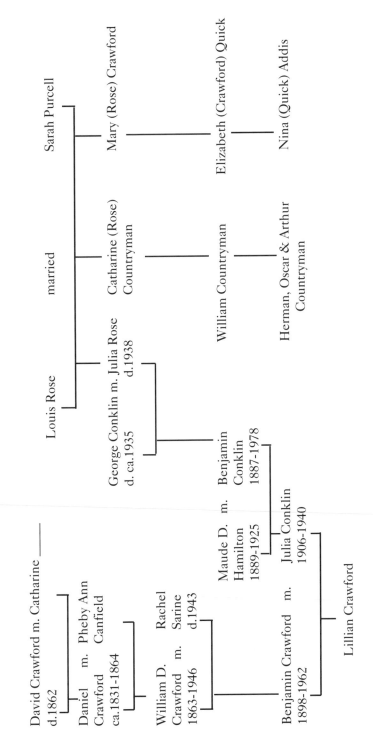

David Crawford m. Catharine _____

Daniel   m.   Pheby Ann
Crawford   Canfield
ca.1831-1864

William D.   Rachel
Crawford   m.   Sarine
1863-1946   d.1943

Maude D.   m.   Benjamin
Hamilton   Conklin
1889-1925   1887-1978

Benjamin Crawford   m.   Julia Conklin
1898-1962   1906-1940

Lillian Crawford

Sarah Purcell

married

Louis Rose

George Conklin m. Julia Rose
d. ca.1935   d.1938

Mary (Rose) Crawford

Catharine (Rose)
Countryman

William Countryman

Herman, Oscar & Arthur
Countryman

Elizabeth (Crawford) Quick

Nina (Quick) Addis

117

Hamilton. She eventually divorced Ben, left Bill for the second time, and married Ernest Bollin. Maude died in a fire at her home on Route 209, just across the Beer Kill bridge from downtown Ellenville. According to the story Lillian heard, "she was cleaning bedsprings with kerosene or gasoline, one or the other, and she lit a match and it ignited and sat her clothes on fire."

Julia was raised mostly by Ben's mother (after whom she was named) and was present as a child at the Five-Mile Post, where Florence (Slover) Pitkin remembers her. Ben's mother was born Julia Rose. One of her seven sisters was the maternal grandmother of Nina Addis. Another was the mother of Bill Countryman. Ben Conklin and Bill Countryman were thus first cousins, and Lillian was, arguably, a second cousin once removed to Nina and to Herman, Art, and Oscar Countryman. Lillian told me her mother used to say she "had no father," but Lillian always considered Ben Conklin to be her grandfather.

As a teenager and young man, Ben Conklin summered at the Five-Mile Post. The family lived in Napanoch and had occasionally picked on Jacob's Ladder. According to a story that Lillian was told by Ben, it was there that Ben's only sister, Laura, got separated from the family while picking berries, at the age of eight, and was never seen again. The berrypickers combed the mountain but never turned up a clue to her fate. Ben was at Sam's Point in the 1920s; he moved thence to the Three-Mile Post and later to the Two-Mile Post, before returning to Sam's Point in the forties.

Lillian's father, Ben Crawford, was a carpenter and mason by trade; during his youth he had worked on neighborhood dairy farms. Every fall and winter Ben hunted raccoons, from 1920 until about 1936, after which "there wasn't any money for coon fur no more," Lillian told me. The family started spending their summers up at Sam's Point about the time Lillian was born. Her father sold his berries to Fritz Lutz in the 1920s, to Joe Roe during 1932 and '33, and later to Art Smith and Paul Gunsch. Sometimes he would bring the family's berries directly to the public market at Newark, New Jersey or to a market in Newburgh. Lillian wrote me the following in a letter describing her youth:

> *My mother and I would go fishing with my father some times. We all was out doors people. My mother loved to take walks in a moon light night and hike in the woods days she wasn't working. We all loved the mountains. It didn't make if Dad had a job or not, when Huckelberries was ripe he quit and went Camping, he made more money picking berries.*
>
> *I think if you went back you would find out that among the oldest campers at Sam's Point would be my Grand-Mother Maude's mother and father Delbert and Ann Donnelly.*

An early berry buyer was Bob Cruver, who was born about 1875 and lived to be ninety-three years of age. Lillian recalls that Cruver loved the mountain and used to talk to her about having picked berries on Sam's Point even during his youth. I spoke with Bob Cruver's daughter Edith Marl, who was born in 1900: She told me her father was buying huckleberries at Sam's Point from the time of her earliest recollection. Bob's father, James, was from Walker Valley; Bob lived in Rockland County as a young man, spending his summers on the mountain, and moved back to the area soon after Edith was born.

They lived for many years in the hamlet of Crawford, virtually in the shadow of Sam's Point. Edith's father had a little store up amongst the pickers' cabins. He would market his berries in Newburgh, making the overnight trip from Sam's Point three or four times a week with his team of horses. Cruver's last year as a buyer was 1922, when his wife, Lorinda, died. He subsequently moved to Florida, but returned every summer to his Sam's Point cabin, just to be on the mountain. He was a blacksmith by trade, and according to Greg Greer, Sr. of Walker Valley, he had a special knack for tempering iron. "Bob Cruver was the best blacksmith in the valley," Greg told me.

Edith mentioned the names of two other men who she recalls bought berries from the pickers on Sam's Point during about the same years as her father. These were brothers Lut Howell from Ellenville and Ace Howell from Ulsterville. Lillian remembers well another buyer, from her own childhood years, Fritz (Fred) Lutz. He had three sons, Charles, Henry, and Fritz, Jr. They all picked huckleberries on Sam's Point, though the sons were only day visitors. Together they owned a general store in Pine Bush. "Just pass the gate on the turn is where Lutz had a cabin. He bought berries before I was born, this I know by my father telling me." Fritz Lutz, Sr. spoke with a heavy German accent. When the berrypickers would all start returning with their harvest at the end of the day, Lutz's familiar refrain, remembers Lillian, was "By Dee-EE-zus, here dey all come!"

> *I always used to call him "Grandpa Lutz." He had what they call a "Ready Reckoner," of berrypickin', like they used to have. It's a book and tells the prices of berries, you know, of so many quarts, and how much and all that. I was pretty good in math as a child, so he used to look over at me and say "Lillian, how much do I owe them?" So I could tell him, without even looking at the book.*
>
> *I can remember at one time, I picked forty-seven and a pint, my mother picked sixty-some quarts, and my father I know picked a hundred and two quarts. And Charlie Lutz, that same day, picked a hundred and six or a hundred and sixteen quarts, I can't be sure which. It had to be back, say, 1930 or '31, somewheres around that era. I was only seven or eight years old. We had written these amounts onto a board in the cabin that we lived in at Sam's Point.*

When Lillian was two years old, she and her parents moved from Ulsterville to the Roosa Gap and Pleasant Valley area in the town of Mamakating, not far from her grandfather's land. Here they used to pick berries on Craine Mountain and Slymer (or Slimmer) Fields during July and then move up to a cabin at Sam's Point as the berries ripened higher up. "Craine

Mountain" denotes the first portion of the ridge northeast of the Route 17 crossing, Slymer Fields are the level areas in a saddle in the Shawangunk ridge, at the highest point along a trail that crosses the mountain between Pleasant Valley and Phillipsport. There were campgrounds at both of these locations, as well as at the horseshoe on the old wagon road above Spring Glen, half a mile below its junction with modern Route 52. Families camped mostly in tents, and what tarpaper shanties there were consisted of very temporary structures that generally lasted only a season. Between Slymer Fields and the horseshoe was Tuttle Hill, where the Ulster-Sullivan county line crosses the mountain. This was the closest good berrypicking for the folks who camped at the horseshoe. Lillian's family camped at Slymer Fields through July 1930 and at Craine Mountain through July 1935. By then most of the pickers had left these areas, which were getting overgrown, since no one set fires here the way they did up on Sam's Point and along the Smiley Road.

Lillian wrote me this concerning her childhood years in the Sullivan County Shawangunks:

> *The La Forge family goes way back in camping and picking berries, John La Forge was a old man in his 80s when he camp at Slymer Fields. I always like him, he was a jolly person. We always had a bon fire going for the bugs and one night I went out and I put a old inner tube of my Fathers on it and almost sat his camp on fire, all the people ran for water and got it out. I was sorry and feeled bad about doing it, but my Mother gave me a good slaping fore it, I never did that again. All of us kids called him Grandpa La Forge. He took me on his knee and talk to me as I was crying after, he said to me go wash your tiers away and go to bed and forget about it, that is what I am going to do.*

John La Forge's son Gus camped with his family at Sam's Point during the 1920s, '30s, and early '40s, Lillian wrote. "He played a little on the fiddle, he also was a basket weaver, he sold his baskets to the berrie pickers and also tours that came up on week ends and wanted to pick a few berries themselfs. His [second] wife Cloe was killed in a car accident 1942 Thanksgiving day." Gus had a son named Senior, a nephew Frank, whom he raised as his own, and a daughter Jennie, whom Lillian and I visited in 1983, when she was well into her seventies. Lillian said there was also a Tom La Forge, who camped with his family in the early 1920s at Sam's Point. He was a cousin of Gus.

Lillian wrote down for me this story about a boy named Lawrence Smith, who came from Napanoch:

> *When Larry was fourteen his father John Smith beat him so bad he ran a way and just was buming around Ellenville. And he was in the store my Father was in, buying food for are selfs and the Campers, he came up to Dad and ask him for money to buy some thing to eat. He told my Dad his story what happen and Dad could see he was hurt and was in pain so he said as soon as I am done I'll talk to you. He waited for Dad and help him carry the things out to the truck. I don't know what all Dad said to him but he bough him back with him. Mom clean his cuts and bannage him up and gave him something to rub on his legs and back and feed him.*
>
> *He stayed and after a few days went picking with us, but he didn't care about picking, we would fine him laying on a large rock up on Tuttle hill. He took a liking to Grandpa Crawford and went down to help with the haying.*
>
> *When the summer was over he took off and it was a long time before we heard from him, then I got a post card from him, no address, mail from Virginia, all it say he was fine and not to worry about him and he ask about us all. I got a card now and then from him they were from all over the Southern states.*

One day when I was 12 years old down helping Grandpa raking hay, Grandma call us for Lunch and after lunch Grandpa took my tea cup to read my tea leaves. He said a young man is going to be coming up the road soon looking for you. I laugh at him and said you didn't see that in my tea cup and he said well you'll see, I said I don't know any one looking for me so he joked around or I took it as a joke, but about two hours after a young man did come up the road and I said Grandpa I think I know him. He went up to Uncle Charley's and visit him for a while and just as we were eating Supper a nock came to the door and I went to answer it and was pulled in Larry's arms.

I was so happy to see him and grandma said its are little Larry but he wasn't little no more he was 19teen then. He was like a big brother to me. He told us some of his life traving around, Mom & Dad came after me and they were glad to see him. He came back with us to Sam's Point, he pick berries enough to keep himself and after a week or so he went to Ellenville and we didn't hear from him till he married Marion Coutant.

He and Marion pick some berries at the two mile Post when they didn't have any work, Marion did house work and Larry done window washing for the stores around Ellenville. We were good friends allways. He would visit us afton and my husband liked him.

He died when he was 47 years old he wasn't a well person, he had weak kidneys from a small boy. His Father did come looking for him but none of the campers would tell him were he was, I guess he didn't care enough to report him missing. By the time Larry came back to Ellenville to stay his Father was dead.

Chapter 10

Of Times Good and Bad
(and Tales True and Tall)

For two years, about 1928 and '29, Lillian's father, Ben Crawford, owned a saw mill rig and, together with his brother Abe and a brother-in-law, leased a wood lot on the mountainside just above Walker Valley, a little southwest of Route 52. "They sold the wood by the cord and made money to keep three families going," Lillian wrote me.

> My father bought a new Model A when they first came out for $750.00. This was in the Depression, we didn't have it hard or go with out like most other people in thoes days, Dad also worked for some well to do people and they had children that had a girl that when she out grow her clothing they would give them to him, I went to school with silk, satin and velvet dresses, also a teddy bear coat, hat and scarf to match. My cousin would say I don't see how your Father can aford to buy you the things you ware and would try and tear my dress also would put gum on my seat so when I sat down I would get it on my dress, an till this day they don't know were I got my clothing that I wore the first year I started school, 1930.

The winter of 1931 Dec. 2nd are house burned down, we lost just about everything and stayed with friends Lillian & Floyd Smith ("Cap" Louis Weed Sr.'s daughter) for a short time, then we moved in Dad's Aunt Mary Crawford Scott's house in Walker Valley, we had sickness, Dad was put in the Hospital and I got a Kidney infection and was sick the rest of the winter so we had are share of bad luck, but we had good friends around Walker Valley and it wasn't long and we were back on are own again. I will always remember all the nice things that the people in Walker-Valley gave me at Christmas that year.

"Come summertime, on Sam's Point," writes Lillian, "the Stedners always had a little store, or you could order fresh meat from them. And we'd have wieny roasts or marshmellows roasted, and to me it was a good time. The menfolks, if they didn't want to join us kids or the womenfolks, they would go and play cards somewheres. Maybe just for penny ante, maybe five and ten but that's all." Occasionally Lillian and some of the others would journey over the mountain to the Smiley Road camps and she'd visit her grandpa Ben Conklin at the Three-Mile Post. The menfolk might hike up to Nina Addis's to have a drink or two.

About the early 1940s the Stedners got a beer license, but Lillian says there was still relatively little drinking among the Sam's Point crowd, compared to what went on at the Smiley Road camps. "Sam's Point was more, people that come there to pick to make a living and to save some money. Not just to have a good time, to get drunk and fight like on the Ellenville side of the mountain. We worked hard and put in long hours to save are money to have nice things for are homes. And jobs was hard in the winter so we layed away and some times we ran a store bill to Lutz's store in Pine Bush that we payed in the summer."

Lillian told me that the road north from Lake Maratanza was not put through all the way to the High Point fire tower until about 1933 or '34. Prior to that time you could take a horse and

12

buggy about one-quarter way there and had to continue on foot. Lillian remembers the crew that built the road to completion:

> *There was thirty-two CC guys, and I have got to say, they were the nicest fellows I think I ever met. Nothing fresh about them. Their boss used to take them off of the mountain once a week to the movies. If they wanted to go in the saloon, if they wanted to get drunk, that was up to them. He waited somewheres around Ellenville, picked them all up, whether they were drunk or not, brought them back. They had their tents, and, like a big chuck wagon, that they had, way in the back of some of the berrypickers' shacks. This was at the end of a lane on the left, just up from the gatehouse.*

The Civilian Conservation Corps also rebuilt the road around the lake. Previous to this improvement, the road was scarcely more than a wagon trail, remembers Lillian.

In 1936 Lillian's family moved across the mountain to Summitville. Later Lillian moved to Ellenville after convalescing in Middletown from a tragic automobile accident on the mountain in 1940 that had taken the life of her mother. While living in Ellenville, Lillian married Martin Wood. During the summertime the couple stayed at the Sam's Point cabin, Lillian picking huckleberries while her husband worked days in Ellenville. Lillian continued thus at Sam's Point from 1943 through most of the summer of 1951.

Lillian was always close with the Countryman family. "Bill Countryman wasn't bad as some people has painted him," she wrote me.

> *He had a good heart. He took a boy in his home and keep him for three years. His name was Matty Bell from Kingston. Matty camp with Bill at Slymer Fields in 1930. He was a good boy and allways helping some one, he was are water boy, he liked going to the Spring. My Uncle Abe had a camp near the Spring and Matty liked him and visit him a lot.*

In February of 1943, Lillian came and stayed with Bill for a few weeks, to help care for him when he had taken ill with a bad cold. The twins were away in the military service at the time. "I know of a family that lived near him in Granit," she wrote. "They would send there girls down to Bill's every day buming for food and Bill would give them.

> *I was waiting for some one to come to get me to go back to Ellenville, the girls came with a note and on it was there Father had the nerve to ask for tobacco, I gave the girls some things and wrote a note that he had a Hell of a nerve to ask a old man for tobacco yet, it is bad enough you send your girls for food all winter, get off of your lazy ass and go to work and keep your own family. I was told after I left Bill's that the children was taken away and he was sent to prison and died in prison. I liked the girls and would bake cake or pie and they would eat it with me befor they went home. I still have there pictures they gave me.*

Lillian related some more stories from her years at Sam's Point. The first is about two lost boys:

> *Back in the mid 30s there was two boys that got lost in the woods, they were about 7 and 5 years old, Lymon & Edsall Conklin, Edsall Conklin Sr.'s sons. The boys got tired picking berries one day, they seen a field and houses in the vally from were they were picking and desided to go see what was down there. The father hunted and called till he was tired out so he came out and some of the men got a man hunt going but while they were hunting for the boys, the boys went to a house on the Oregen trail road.*
> *The people was very nice and feed them and Lymon was able to tell them they camp with there Father on the mountain. The people didn't know for sure but got the boys in there car and came up to Sam's Point. Stedner's at that time run the gate and let them*

in. The boys was back before the men, waiting for there Father, they had lost there picking pails and little boxes that there Uncle Andy had made for them, and had torden there clothing and cuts from the bush going in the deep woods, but we thank God nothing happen to them other than that.

Lillian's next story concerns a young man who did not camp and pick berries at Sam's Point but who frequently visited a cousin of his who was a summertime resident of the berry camps:

In the late 40s a boy I had knowen sence he was small, a good looking boy and a nice kid to me, he was in the Service at West Point, he came to visit me in a officers unform, I said I see you are doing good for yourself and he said Mom I am, and I like Army life. He kiss me and said I'll see you soon, I and my friend are going to ride around the lake. I didn't think any thing more about it, but not over a half a hour had pass and a Police car from Ellenville and a West Point Army car with two officers was looking for them both. I and my Daughter started to walk down to the gate house store when this boy and his friend came down from the Lake and was going so fast they almost hit us, I had to take the ditch and my Daughter jumped up on the bank to get out of the way, behind them was the Police car and army car. They got them near Walker Valley. They killed a officer and stole his unform, that he was wearing. I don't want to give there names because his relatives all lives around Walden and area, the other boy was a judges son from Sullivan County.

"You see, we had some excitement on Sam's Point," Lillian continued, "also once in a while a driffer would come to the mountains and some of the pickers would have there berries stolen by them, we never had this to happen to us."

A story concerning Lillian's father comes to me from Chet Van Demark (born 1921), who lives in a cabin along Bruyn

Turnpike, near the hamlet of Red Mills in the town of Shawangunk. Chet reports that he heard from his maternal grandfather, Frank Scott (1854-1931), that Ben once swapped a woman he was living with "for a load of hay and a sack of cabbages." Later, says Chet, "Ben ran into the man with whom he had made the swap and asks, 'How ya makin' out with my ex?' 'OK, I finally got the Crawford smell out of her,'" was the reply. The story has all the earmarks of a good-natured joke, which is how Lillian responded to it when, with some trepidation, I asked for her reaction. She said she had heard a story of her father swapping a woman for something or other, but that there was never any truth to it.

Chet's father, Richard, worked as a hired hand at local dairy farms. Chet spent his childhood summers living with his maternal grandparents in their old log cabin on Jones Road, a dead-end lane off Oregon Trail near Walker Valley. He used to pick berries on the mountain on daytime outings. He told me two animal stories he'd heard from his grandfather Frank: Once Frank was returning on foot across the mountain from Ellenville with a quarter of beef that he'd received in trade for a sheep or lamb; he was descending the footpath toward Jones Road from the saddle between Sam's Point and Losees Hill when a bobcat supposedly sprang onto the beef, which he was carrying on his shoulders. Frank reportedly shoved his lantern into the cat's face, which scared it off. Chet surmises it was an older bobcat whose prowess at hunting live game was not what it used to be. Frank and his wife, Martha, had a "summer kitchen" next to the log cabin, an outbuilding that was used during the fall and winter to store smoked meats, dried fruit, and such. One time, according to Chet's grandfather, a bear climbed up on top of this building, attracted by the smell of the food stored inside. It was tearing shakes off the roof, hoping to get in, when his grandmother shot it dead with a muzzle-loader rifle.

When I inquired of Chet whether Frank Scott had a reputation for telling tall tales, Chet did acknowledge that, when he was a young boy, his grandfather used to tell him to walk barefoot through fresh cow manure whenever possible, that it would make his feet grow. Otherwise, warned Frank, if you grow up with small feet, "you'd be sinkin' in the mud all the while and won't be worth a damn!"

Lillian told me of her own encounter with a bear, in the summer of 1952. In the following story, she informs me that the "Bumblebee Swamp" refers to an area east of the Fire Tower Road, not far from its junction with the loop that circles Lake Maratanza:

> *I took a friend back in the woods to pick berries and I came back out, I and my daughter both, to gather up all the German Camp menfolks' grocery orders. But as I was coming out, I don't know what possessed me to look down into the woods, but when I did, I saw this big bear standing right up. And she looked to me as though she was gonna have cubs. And I went down, and my father hadn't left the campground yet to go berrying, and I told him about it, and of course he laughed at me, and as I told it to the rest of the campers when I came back from doing the shopping, they also laughed at me about it. But a few days later my father and a few other of the campers, Ernie Williams and his wife Mary for one, was picking berries and Mrs. Williams was chased by the bear and lost her shoe in the swamp. I seen some of the campers were out, and I was wondering why, and I went down to my father's camp and he had kind-ee a silly grin on his face and when I seen that I sure knew that something had happened. So I said to him "What, did ya's all go in the Bumblebee Swamp today and was chased by the bear?" He says "You've got it; ask Mary where her shoe is."*

Lillian described a wildlife sighting she experienced about four years prior to seeing the bear: She was walking toward the cliff along a footpath that left the road opposite the Van Leuvens' cabin (later Herman Heigle's), on the road up from the gatehouse. About halfway between the road and the cliff, a mountain lion jumped across the path from left to right, only about twenty-five feet in front of her, Lillian reports. She saw

Lillian Crawford Wood at Sam's Point, ca. 1952.

the whole length of its body, including the tail. She estimates it might have weighed seventy-five pounds. Lillian said that Herman Heigle had told her he'd seen a long-tailed cat the same year he bought from the Van Leuvens, which was 1963. (A native of southern Germany, Herman was a member of the German settlement on Sam's Point. He retired from food-service work in New York City and became a year-round dweller in his Sam's Point cabin in 1966. He was the last surviving Sam's Point resident. Herman died of a stroke in January 1983, aged seventy-six.)

In August 1951, Lillian separated from her husband (who died five years later) and moved from Ellenville to Phillipsport. During the summers of 1952 through '54 she camped at Sam's Point intermittently, rather than all summer long. Thereafter she visited the mountaintop only on weekend day visits.

Lillian moved to Summitville in the fall of 1954. "In Summitville," writes Lillian, "I worked out doing house work and took in boarders to make ends meet and put my daughter through school. My father boarded with us for a while, also he had a small house trailer parked on the lot by me, he sold it and was living at Walden when he went up to Sam's Point to fix the camp and died up there alone, of a heart attack, March 1962. My father was to give my daughter away in marriage, I had his suit cleaned but buried him in it instead."

Art McFarland of Ellenville gives this account of the death of Ben Crawford:

> *Me, Ben, and Floyd Williams used to live together in Walden. Ben went up to Sam's Point to fix the roof on his cabin. He was gone the weekend, he was supposed to be back Sunday evening, and he didn't show up. So Monday evening we went up to look for him. We found his car at the gate, we went up to his shack, I opened the door and there lay Ben on the floor. I reached down and took his hand, but he was dead.*

From time to time during the fourteen years she rented out rooms to boarders, Lillian took in local youths from troubled homes. It is a source of pride and satisfaction to her that she was able to help many of these boys find work and straighten up their lives. For the most part she succeeded in earning both their respect and affection. She also rented a room to an old friend, Art Countryman, and tried her best to keep him away from the bottle. He boarded with Lillian for thirteen years. "Art would go sometimes maybe six months to a year and wouldn't touch anything," Lillian said. "And then he would go off on a tear that. . . you couldn't *get* him off of it."

Lillian was willing to come to Art's defense when he needed help, as evidenced by this story she told me of an appearance before Judge Lonstein of Ellenville about 1958:

> *I went to pick up Arthur from work one night and he wasn't there, so I went and asked his boss, and his boss said that he had left and he didn't know where he was. So I said to him "Could it be possible that he was picked up by the police?" As he called the police station, sure enough, there is where he was. They had picked him up for—he said—stumbling and, he fell and, the*

police came along at the same time that he was down, trying to get up, and they picked him up for drunkenness. So I went up and bailed him out, which cost me fifteen dollars, and he was supposed to appear on a certain date back into court.

We went back and he was fined fifteen dollars. So I told the judge "Well, yeah, you pick up him *for stumblin' on the sidewalk," I said "Why didn't you pick up some of the drunks that—when I lived here in Ellenville by the bridge they would open up their pants and pee right offa the bridge," I said, "You didn't come along and pick* them *up, none of the cops," I said.*

Lillian was threatened with a fine for contempt of court and then told angrily to leave the courtroom. A friend, the daughter of Art's sister Luella, later told her she'd have paid Lillian's fine if the judge had found her in contempt, for the pleasure of seeing her tell off the judge and stick up for her Uncle Art!

In the summer of 1959 Art had a job at the Granit Hotel, and Lillian would bring him to work each day from Summitville. She'd then spend the day picking huckleberries on Mary Crose's Mountain, just across the road from the Seiberts (the former Mary Crose house) or sometimes up nearly as far as George Decker's house. At the end of the day, she'd sell these berries directly to the hotel, or at other times to Grace Decker, before picking Art up from work and driving back to Summitville together.

At Sam's Point, from 1956 through 1961, Lillian's commercial huckleberry picking was limited to filling orders that friends or neighbors placed with her. Beginning 1952, she would also earn a few dollars shopping for some of the German folks who still camped there. After 1961, what picking Lillian did was only for her personal use. Her last regular visits to Sam's Point were in 1967.

Chapter 11

In Which Joe Roe
Gets the Last Laugh

A name that has come up frequently in the course of my inquiries among a variety of sources is that of Willard Yorks, a Sam's Point huckleberry picker who wrote songs and played a number of musical instruments, including accordion, violin, guitar, and mouth organ. He also caned chairs and wove baskets, lampshades, and such. His daughter Betty Brown lives in Ellenville as of this writing. Willard Fillmore Yorks was born May 1883 in the hamlet of Crawford (town of Shawangunk), the son of George Yorks and Sarah Elizabeth La Forge. Sarah is believed to have been a sister of John La Forge, whom Lillian Wood remembers from Slymer Fields. Willard camped and picked berries at Sam's Point from the first decade of this century.

It was on Sam's Point that Willard met May Pickford (born January 1885), whom he married in 1910. May's parents, Moses and Elizabeth, both born in the 1850s, were berrypickers and campers at Sam's Point from the turn of the century or earlier. Elizabeth, who died in 1925, was the daughter of Andrew Yorks (no known relation to Willard's family), who died about the early 1920s at the age of 104.

Willard and May were interviewed in their old age by Norman Studer, who collected songs and folklore, mostly from the Catskill region. The following notes on Sam's Point are from the Studer archives, housed in College Hall E-203 at the college in New Paltz:

> *There are two settlements—the German and the American. In the German come city workers, cooks, pastrymen, caterers, longshoremen, to escape the heat of the city and make a few dollars a day while they enjoy the mountain air. Some of them follow the crops for the rest of the summer, going farther north for apple picking when the berry season is over. In the American colony are the native mountain people. Williard York [sic] and his wife are. . . members of the American settlement.*

The German camp made up the last group of berrypickers' shacks, on the level part of the road, well past the present shale quarry.

Some of the people at Sam's Point, mostly among the Germans, called Willard "Huckleberry Bill," though the nickname was not widely used. Studer reproduces one of the many songs Willard wrote:

Huckleberry Bill

In the good old Shawangunk Mountains where the
    huckleberries grow
In the good old summertime, there the berrypickers go
There you will find me, roaming on the hill
That's why they call me Old Huckleberry Bill.

Chorus:
Huckleberry Bill, roaming over the mountain
Huckleberry Bill, the berries for to get
Huckleberry Bill, roaming over the mountain
When the berrypicking's over, you'll find me roaming yet.

When the berrypicking's over and the folks have moved away
I can't resist temptation on that rocky hill to stay
There you will find me roaming over the hill
That's why they call me Old Huckleberry Bill.

Betty (Yorks) Brown told me her father was the original author of the popular song "Blueberry Hill," first a hit in 1940 and later made famous by Fats Domino. She said her father's version was called "Huckleberry Hill"; according to Betty, he sent the words away to a music publishing company and had the song stolen from him. Years ago, Betty saw her father's manuscript, and she says the words were nearly identical to the version that later became a hit.

After Willard and May were married, they settled in Ellenville. Willard was a jack-of-all-trades; he did carpentry and masonry as well as weaving, and on Sam's Point he measured huckleberries for Homer Wynkoop, Art Smith, Grover Perkins, and Paul Gunsch. A little dispute has arisen regarding his berrypicking: One normally reliable source has told me that Willard sometimes used a berry rake and his harvest was full of leaves and twigs. "Paul Gunsch and Grover Perkins would give him hell about this," I was told. Willard's daughter not only denies this, but says her father was a stickler for clean berries, both those he picked himself and those he measured. My other source agrees he was a stickler when it came to other people's berries, but positively sticks to what was said regarding Willard's own picking. It may be that Willard became less meticulous in his later years, during which time his daughter was no longer a regular visitor to Sam's Point.

Willard and May continued camping summers at Sam's Point through about 1953, or '54 at latest, according to Betty. May suffered a serious stroke that confined her to a wheelchair, and neither went up to the mountain after that. After May's death in January 1957, Willard's mind was not right, and he followed her to the grave in April of the next year.

Willard Yorks made Sam's Point his home during half a century of huckleberry seasons. The Shawangunk Mountains were the source of much of the raw material he used for weaving berry baskets and other useful items as well as his source of inspiration for the music he loved to write and play. It was Willard's friends and companions on the mountain who were in large part the beneficiaries of these same varied talents.

The name of Art Smith has been mentioned among those of buyers to whom both Willard Yorks and Ben Crawford sold berries. Art bought huckleberries at Sam's Point from about 1930 until about 1947. His daughter Marie Distel told me that her father, who was born in 1887, used to speak of camping and picking berries at Sam's Point during his childhood, with his own parents, John and Catherine Smith. Marie was born in 1916. She camped with her family at Sam's Point as a young girl, until the time her father started as a buyer. Thereafter she and her mother stayed in Ellenville and Art came to the mountain only as a day visitor, to pick up the berry crates and tend to business. Marie's older brother, Art, Jr., camped at the horseshoe above Spring Glen for several years, where he measured berries for his father. Afterward he moved to Sam's Point, where he continued working for his father until entering the military service about 1942.

Down at the family's home on Chapel Street, southeast of the Sandburg Creek in Ellenville, Marie's mother, Mary Ellen ("Mame"), would measure berries that day pickers brought in. "My father wasn't a person that laughed a lot or was very talkative," Marie told me. "When he was in business he was all business. But my mother, she was just the opposite.

"Most of the berrypickers were local people, neighbors and friends, and a lot of them at that time worked for Ulster Knife. And then they would take the summer off to pick berries." Marie recalls that rattlesnakes were often the subject of conversation: "Sometimes the berrypicker would tell about seein' a rattlesnake that day. The berrypicker, I think that was his biggest fear in the woods was runnin' on a rattlesnake. And if he could kill it he killed it. But sometimes he'd come down and say, well, he saw a great big one, and it would be big, even if he had to stretch the story a little bit."

Two years before her death in 1989, I made the acquaintance of a woman named Viola, a widow who lived on Lower Mountain Road in the town of Shawangunk. She had spent summers camping at Sam's Point in the 1930s and '40s, some years full-time and in later years as a weekend picker.

Viola was born in December 1914, the daughter of Jacob and Minnie (Stokes) Williams. She grew up in Modena and Walden and, while in her teens, married Pete Decker. Through another marriage late in life she became Viola Yanualivic.

The following occurred at Sam's Point when Viola's boy Ray ("Sonny") was about eight or ten, according to Viola. "This one night I had to get up and go to the bathroom. I didn't know my son was out there. My son had been down there and he was comin' between the cabins. I had the flashlight but I didn't have it on, and I felt this, like—hair, you know. Here I'm beatin' him in the head with a flashlight I thought it was a bear after me. And he says 'Ma, Ma, Ma, it's me!' And I says 'Oh my God, Sonny, I thought it was an animal!'" Ray thinks this happened when he was thirteen or fourteen, not eight or ten. "I had a lot of bumps on my head for a while after that," he told me.

Viola kept a pet spider monkey up on the mountain. "I used to take him up huckleberryin' with me. He'd climb up in the bush and he'd eat more berries than I could pick. He got in my pail and upset it a few times. A lot of people took his pictures, they'd set him on their lap and pictures was taken of 'em, I guess there's pictures all over the country of him." Viola says once a Dalmatian came around to the cabin, a fire dog up from Cragsmoor or someplace; the monkey chased the dog out of the yard with a broom. "This dog went kiyitin' out the yard with his tail between his legs and the monkey right after him. I got the monkey back and then I tied him to the limb. And he used to swing on the swing. I had a cat up there, and he used to take the cat's tail and swing the cat back and forth by the tail."

Viola recalled a man named Peg Leg Penny: "He had a wooden leg and a cane and he went up there on the mountain pickin' berries. John Stedner found him froze to death." This was Adam "Penny" Smith, who was found dead one day about the mid 1940s in the little shack where he lived alone, in the woods off upper Pine Street, near the south corner of Ellenville. Marie Distel told me this story about Peg Leg Penny:

There was a colored minister and his wife who lived on Pine Street. And they were very religious people. And Penny Smith came through one night, and he was drunk. And you wondered how he ever stood up on that peg leg, when he was so drunk. And when he got there by their house, the minister and his wife, I guess they figured he needed some help, before he was to meet his maker. So they took him in the house and baptized him right there, in the bathtub. And I guess they kept him until he sobered up. But after that he went right on drinking.

Lillian Wood remembers hearing, as a child, of another man who met his end in the same unfortunate manner as Peg Leg Penny. "He was a friend of my Father's, I don't remember much about him myself. He camp at the Horseshoe and at Sam's Point. It was late 20s or earley 30s, he froze to death in his little house in Phillipsport." In this case, the poor man's fate was perhaps preordained, for his name, as Lillian told me, was Jim Frost.

I had mentioned, in passing, the name Frank "Doodle" Bradford, in connection with the Four-Mile Post. As it turns out, Frank was the maternal uncle of Lillian Wood's husband. "Frank Bradford pick berries on the Ellenville side of the mountain for years," Lillian wrote me.

He merried Lottie Terwilliger. In 1946 when his son George came out of the service they camp up to Sam's Point. I liked Uncle Frank and feel sorry for George, he had nerves spells he like to be alone a lot, some times I could get him to play his Gutar for me and would talk with us, it was awfull what the wor did too him He was such a good boy and a good looking young man and could of had a life, but the wor made him so he lived a lonley life.

Frank was always whittling on something, Lillian said. He made all sorts of wood carvings, decorative plaques, dollhouse furniture, etc., and Lillian thinks his nickname might derive from this hobby. "He was a jolly person to be around, but he did not care much about working."

Doodle Bradford, Peg Leg Penny, Jerk Vandermark, Duckfoot—I will confess to a certain fascination with authentic nicknames; these, among others, have lodged in my mind, where they persist in arousing a stubborn curiosity about the souls and bodies to which they belong. So it was that when I heard from a number of folks about a couple of gals from Ellenville with a particularly uproarious nickname, which they shared in common, I grew determined to learn more. Although they were not berrypickers, nor were they associated directly with life on the mountain, the women, long deceased, were known to so many of the folks whose stories I have told that, indeed, I would be remiss to omit telling something of their own history.

These two ladies weighed in at about a quarter ton apiece. "They were happy-go-lucky people," one woman told me, "they would help anybody that needed help. They always had a big smile for people and they always spoke to everybody, they never thought they were any better than anybody else."

Although they had many friends and even paramours, and no one ever suggested that their personalities were anything but amiable, fastidiousness was apparently not their style: The state of both their domestic and somatic realms drew painful winces of recollection from a Smiley Road berrypicker who himself had been reared in circumstances that were anything but palatial; another told me the two women kept chickens caged right within their living quarters and that she even saw the chickens ranging at will through the house on at least one occasion. The women lived for a long time on Bender (now "Tow Path") Street, between Center and Canal, southeast of the Sandburg. Their last place of residence was near "the Points," where Center and Canal Streets join at the northwest edge of Ellenville.

It seems that a common nickname is not all they shared, for they were inseparable companions throughout their lives. Nina

Addis told me, "They always came together as a pair. If a man took up with one of them, he had to take the sister in with the bargain." And sisters (in the literal, biological sense) are what the two women were always understood to be, for they shared a common surname and had grown up together under the same roof. But one informant, who has been the source of much reliable information, claims otherwise: "My mother knew them in Napanoch before they moved to Ellenville, and I know for a fact that they were mother and daughter," I was told. My source recalled for me, from the age of about fourteen, a specific discussion that had taken place, and related to me in considerable detail its locus, context, and content.

Recently I came across another individual, apparently in a position to know, who confirmed this information for me. But since originally none of the women's other acquaintances would support the notion, I had decided to see if I could clear up the matter through a study of vital records. The elder woman was born June 1883 and died in 1957. The younger lacks a birth registry—which in itself is possibly somewhat suspicious—but her death record, dated 1955, shows she was born April 1896. This indicates that approximately twelve years and ten months separated them in age, certainly a slim differential, but far from unlikely in terms of biological capabilities.

The death registry records the same parents for the two, but it must be understood that this sort of information would have generally been entered without contention on the basis of information provided by next of kin. And if the survivor of the two (the older woman, as it happens) had spent her life perpetuating a small deception, there is no reason to suppose that she'd have come clean for the sake of posterity.

I returned to the birth record of the older woman and noted a salient piece of information: The age of her parents at her birth was given as forty and sixty respectively for her mother and father. This would mean that if they were in fact sisters, as they claimed all their lives, their mother would have been between fifty-two and ten months and fifty-three and ten months of age at the birth of her youngest daughter. While not quite impossible, this is biologically improbable enough so as to nearly clinch the case for a mother-daughter relationship.

I say nearly, not absolutely, for in the end, is not certain proof of almost anything an elusive goal? And so, in the interest of discretion, I'll close my summation without seeking a final verdict and conclude by saying that I sincerely hope my little investigation has not disturbed the quiet slumbers of these two citizens of Ellenville. Ah yes, there is the matter of their nickname: These inseparable ladies were known to Ellenville and all the world as "the Mud Turtle Twins."

Lillian Wood delved into her store of memories and provided me with additional names and reminiscences from her years on the mountain:

Jess & Lora Mack from near Crawford camp at Sam's Point, Mom would leave me with Lora when I was a baby till I was 4 or 5 years old now & then. Lora had tuberculosis and some times she wasn't able to do much of any thing, then Mom would have to take me with her in the berry woods. Lora pass away at a young age I don't think she was any older than 28 or 29 years old. I loved her and cryed when she was gone, I still think of her. Jess remerried not to long after Lora died to Sarah Bennett and went to Ellenville to live, he drove up to Sam's Point on week ends or when he wasn't working.

Lillian writes that John Smith, a carpenter from Ellenville, was a weekend day picker for many years, before he and his wife, Rose, a sister of Sarah (or "Sally") Bennett, built a cabin on Sam's Point and camped there for the summers of 1936-39. There were thirteen Bennett children. Besides Rose and Sally there were brothers Sike, John, and Charles and a sister Gertrude.

Sike Bennett and family came up on week ends, just to get out of Ellenville for the Summer in the late 40s and earley 50s. Also John Bennett, he didn't pick berries he just like to be by him self and get out of the heat of Ellenville, it was awfull hot in the valley. I know I was always glad to get out of the village and be back up on the mountain were there was a breez most of the time.

Charles ("Choke") Bennett had the store and tollgate at Sam's Point during later years, Lillian wrote, "till Ellenville got a smart idea of changing its name to Ice Cave Mountain." At the store "you could buy most any kind of food, we had fresh bake goods, a baker truck came up, and fruit peddler couple times a week."

I visited Sally (Bennett) Mack and her older sister Gertrude (Bennett) Tremper in their Ellenville home. They were born in 1910 and 1904 respectively. They told me their father, Willington ("Wick") Bennett, who died about the 1920s, had worked for many years at the Sun Ray Bottling Company; his job was pushing the little tourist train that followed tracks into the old "Spanish Tunnel" to the wishing well at the far end, over five hundred feet into the mountain. Gertrude told me the visitors were seated single file, four or five to the train, and on the return trip, with a slight downhill grade, Wick could hop on the back and enjoy a free ride back out.

I have mentioned the Williams and Towne families in connection with the Two-Mile Post. The Williamses moved to Sam's Point for their berrypicking; one of the sons, Floyd, was a friend of Ben Crawford. George Towne likewise moved to Sam's Point in the 1940s, he bought and marketed berries for a while. Lillian remembers he had a small flatbed truck that he'd fabricated by welding a truck bed onto the back of an old passenger car from which he'd cut the rear body off. Lillian continues with her list of Sam's Point pickers:

There were George Bilyou, he had three sons, George Jr., Frank, and Billy. Also William Bilyou, who I think was an uncle to George Sr. This William and his family camped and bought berries in 1948. They had two kids, Sylvia and Douglas. Also there was Russel, Henry, and

Roy Babcock, brothers, and their sister Rita, all originally from New Jersey. Roy and his wife Sally lived in Sparrow Bush, N.Y., near Port Jervis. They camped up where the c.c.c. camp was, and kept coming up till the mid '50s. It was Russel Babcock that help me get my car down off a big rock, I jumped the ditch and the car went on a rock, I was learning to drive on a old 1941 Hudson. This was 1952.

Also there was a family named Heady from Spring Valley and White Plains, there was a Nodgee Heady, Walter, and Eugene Heady who was a cousin of Walter. Also a girl nicknamed Red Sarah that married a Conklin. Also Bill Corwin, known as "Whiskey Bill," born and raised in Summitville. He was a bit of a drifter, he picked berries up there on and off during the '30s. Also some of the Rugers, Jean Ruger merried Roy Bacon and they camp in 1952. There were Jim and Nick Donely, Nick last camp 1944 or 45. Also Ruth Teller & children one year, she was a sister of my Father's. Charley Scott & family camp in the late 40s at Sam's Point, his wife Amelia was also my Father's sister.

I remember one year in the mid 30s a large family called Heigel all played some kind of music. Some of the old campers got a barn dance going out in the field and sang old songs. Many years pass and no one heard from any of them till 1948, then Ralph Heigel and his wife Ruth came up to Sam's Point and camped off and on till 1959.

In the fall of 1969, Lillian moved into a trailer in Summitville and ceased taking in boarders, though Art Countryman continued to stay with her till the following spring. She moved to Port Jervis in July 1971, to a job in Massachusetts in '74, and in 1975 moved upstate, to be closer to her family.

Despite her increasing difficulty in remaining ambulatory, for many years Lillian nearly always managed to make an annual trip down to the Shawangunk region to spend a week with one or another of her cousins or old friends. I'd always spend some time with her, and on one occasion I brought her over for a visit with Nina Addis, whom she'd not seen in six or seven years. In September 1983, during one of Lillian's visits to the area, she decided she'd like to look in on Joe Roe, who'd been a huckleberry buyer on Sam's Point for a time during Lillian's childhood. As we rode up the mountain on Roosa Gap Road, Lillian told me a little story concerning Joe. This she recalled as having happened one evening up at Sam's Point during the summer of 1932, when the pickers were customarily receiving ten cents a quart for their berries:

> *My mother and father came out of the woods, and myself, and Mr. Roe says "All we're paying tonight is eight cents a quart." My mother says "Well if that's all you're paying," she says, "I'll take all these berries and stomp them under my feet." Joe laughed and he says "Oh, we're givin' ten cents yet to ya."*

We found Joe Roe sitting in a chair outside his house, drinking a beer. Lillian called him over to the car. It had been fourteen years since they had seen each other, and Lillian immediately whispered to me how much Joe had aged. About thirty seconds of one-sided banter passed, during which Lillian tried to extract some sign of recognition from this man, who had been such a familiar figure during her youth. Just as we were wondering whether, at seventy-eight, Joe's memory might not be equal to the task, he spoke up for the first time and, with a perfectly straight face, said: "We're only payin' four cents tonight, Lilly." Needless to say, there wasn't a straight face among us after that!

Epilogue

Perhaps the time has come to describe berrypicking as it might be practised today and, first off, to discuss the terms *huckleberry* and *blueberry* and tackle the question of what difference there be between the one and the other. That there is most assuredly a difference is well known to botanists, but the truth may come as something of a surprise to those who have picked or eaten the berries all their lives and not even known which it was they were *not* eating: All the edible, more or less blue-hued wild berries that I've dauntlessly referred to as huckleberries are, strictly speaking, not huckleberries at all, but rather blueberries. Included among the blueberries are both low-bush and high-bush species, with all their multitudinous variety in size, color, and texture of both leaf and fruit. These belong to the genus *Vaccinium*, whereas the huckleberry is of the genus *Gaylussacia*.

My use of the "wrong" word when speaking in other than a scientific context has not (you may be sure) been unintentional. For language is not the private property of scholars, and I am following common usage as practised among those who have, in this case, perhaps more right than any others to define these terms: the berrypickers themselves. They'd have given no serious argument to anyone wishing to call the fruit "blueberries," and indeed some of them occasionally and interchangeably called it this themselves. But the word they employed much more commonly was *huckleberry*, with *blueberry* usually reserved to denote the cultivated version.

Checking a venerable tome from my bookcase, Neltje Blanchan's *Nature's Garden*,[1] I read that

> *The name huckleberry, which is applied indiscriminately to several species of* Vaccinium *and* Gaylussacia,. . . *is evidently a corruption of whortleberry. Whortleberry is in turn a corruption of myrtleberry. In the Middle Ages, the true myrtleberry was largely used in cookery and medicine, but the European bilberry or* Vaccinium *so closely resembled it that the name was transferred to the latter plant. . . . From the European whortleberry the name was transferred to the similar American plants.*

In such manner does language often evolve.

There is another shrub that bears very dark bluish fruit and that is extremely common on the mountaintop. It grows about two or three feet high, having leaves of a light green, almost yellowish green color that turn brilliant maroon-red in early fall. Its berries are sweet enough to the taste, but each contains ten hard seeds (actually nutlets or pits, each containing a seed). These are a little too large to ignore and too small and numerous to bother spitting out, the berry consequently being near worthless to humans. One or two persons have told me these "crackerberries"—as they are called by the huckleberry pickers—are poisonous. But any malaise that may be attributed to eating large quantities of them is apparently due merely to the indigestion that comes from swallowing the pits.

Some years ago a young naturalist from the Mohonk Preserve distinguished for me the true huckleberries from the blueberries of the mountain. It was he who first informed me that all the edible ones are really blueberries. There is only one species on the mountain that is properly called "huckleberry," he told me, and it is very common. He pointed to a nearby shrub: He was pointing to a crackerberry bush!

For a time after first exploring the Smiley Road in 1962, I was attracted to the idea of picking huckleberries (blueberries)

[1] New York: Doubleday, Page & Company, 1907

147

myself, for my own consumption. But it never seemed to be worth the toil: Returning to my car after a summer day at one of the swimming holes on the Peters Kill, I'd sometimes linger to gather berries, but after fifteen or twenty minutes I'd have only a cupful. I'd drive home, pour them into a bowl with evaporated milk, and in a minute or two they'd be gone. To drive to the mountain and hike all the way in to the prime berrying grounds for the privilege of bending over for several hours in the summer heat always seemed an idea which, if acted upon, would be sure to lead to disillusionment. And I had the distinct impression anyway that the berries did not grow as thickly as they used to.

During most of the 1960s and '70s, it was Shawangunk's topography and natural history that most engaged me: I prospected for crystals in the mountain's ancient mine holes, rock-hopped up or down along its tumbling streambeds, climbed among the talus slopes, crisscrossed the pine barrens, and traversed every lofty escarpment, scanning the broad valleys and distant blue horizons that seem to stretch out before the eye to infinity. I built a small, sturdy cabin amid the glorious isolation of the Badlands, where I bathed in the summer sun, kept company round a glowing fire at high winter, enjoyed the tumults of the atmosphere, observed the flowers and trees of the forest, encountered the wild creatures, and listened to the sounds of the wind.

It was not until 1980 that a renewed acquaintance with the people and history of the Smiley Road piqued my curiosity about picking huckleberries, and I decided the next summer to walk the length of the road, picking berries along the way; to complete the nostalgic flavor of the outing, I'd spend a night in Blacky's cabin, something I'd been meaning to do for some time. As it turns out, I was fortunate to have gone that year, for by the following summer the cabin was in ruins.

A teenage friend of mine, who loved the mountain even as I, joined me for the two-day outing, which happily coincided with an invigorating spell of brisk weather, during the second week of August. At the Two- and Three-Mile posts we were hard-pressed to find berries of any consequence—we managed a little desultory picking, just for the fun of having our harvest "cross-pollinated," as it were, by a sampling of fruit from each of the several camps. At the Four-Mile Post, to our delight, the berries were plentiful enough for us to hunker down for what we considered serious picking. By suppertime we'd collected several quarts between us.

The next morning my friend and I set out for the long walk to Lake Awosting and the Minnewaska Trail. Scarcely a minute along our way, we were stopped dead in our tracks by the sight of lush high-bush blueberries crowding close upon the road. Our exertions of the previous day seemed laughable when compared to the bounty offered by these king-sized bushes. We harvested more from the large swale that crosses the road five minutes beyond Polack Camp and from the bushes along the shores of Lake Awosting, and we went home with the happy feeling of having had an adventure and accomplished a goal.

It was thus I learned the secret of success in modern-day Shawangunk Mountain huckleberrying: the high-bush berries, or "swampberries" as the old-time pickers call them (though they often grow in places that would hardly qualify as swamps). The low-bush huckleberries were once the mainstay of the berry industry, but this was due in large part to the fact that they begin ripening early in the season and continue bearing fruit for many weeks. They also commanded a higher price than the late-season swampberries, a consideration irrelevant to the picker interested in home consumption. I freeze my berries and use them in pancakes and cereal the year-round, so it makes not a whit of difference whether my year begins and ends in early July or mid August. Furthermore, it is the low-bush berries that have suffered most from the lack of fires in recent decades and the crowding out of the berry grounds with higher-growing shrubs and trees. The high-bush berries' natural habitat is in shady areas, and their greater height makes them less vulnerable to the inroads of competing vegetation. They are also less affected by the vicissitudes of weather, whereas the low-growing varieties often dry up after a severe

July heat wave. In more than a dozen years of gathering an annual berry harvest, including a few summers with serious heat and drought, I have never seen the high-bush crop seriously diminished by summer weather—although in 1987 a Memorial Day heat wave was the apparent cause of the near-total failure of pollination that canceled the blueberry harvest through wide areas of the Northeast.

Additional advantages of no little import are the larger size of the fruit, their greater ease of harvest, and the fact that the swampberries ripen at a time when the worst heat of the season is past; it is thus possible to enjoy a measure of physical comfort unlikely to be experienced during a July outing. The berries reach their peak of ripeness during the middle third of August at the higher elevations. I always await a break in the summer heat and have never been disappointed. One year I needed to delay my trip until the twentieth of the month, not late enough to significantly affect the harvest. But any later than that, one risks taking home some of those little white worms Nina Addis once warned me about.

When that first hint of autumn arrives, with nighttime temperatures in the forties or fifties and daytime highs well below eighty, I am off with my backpack, in which I carry plastic containers with tight-fitting lids. For picking I use a half-gallon juice container whose handle straps firmly to my belt and whose mouth is the right size for letting berries in and keeping twigs and leaves out. On a few occasions I've done my berrypicking on a day trip or two, but more commonly I bring a tent and sleeping bag: I set a leisurely pace, picking five or six hours on the first and second day and hiking out the third day at whatever time my pack reaches capacity. About fifteen to twenty-five quarts covers my yearly consumption and is a quantity that can be packed out without undue strain.

In 1982 I returned to the Smiley Road for my berrypicking, but thereafter I realized it made more sense to accumulate my bounty at a single campsite rather than having to pack it with me along the length of the road. So the following year I set up camp in the Indian Cave and picked around Mud Pond during the mornings, then stashed my berries in the shade back near the cave and did my afternoon picking at Lake Awosting, where I'd enjoy a swim and take some drinking water back with me at day's end.

In the years since then, I have often camped at a favorite spot at the south corner of the Badlands, about a twenty minute hike from the Verkeerder Kill. But I've occasionally chosen to set up my tent at other locations, such as the exposed 2060-foot plateau above Ann's Spring, half a mile west-northwest of the Five-Mile Post, or the rocky knoll overlooking the inner curve of a beaver pond southwest of Mud Pond.

These sites command magnificent views and allow me to fill all my storage containers without wandering farther than a few minutes from my tent. Each afternoon I'll knock off "work" at four o'clock or so, secure my berries, and set off for a refreshing dip or shower before returning to camp for supper. I'll end the day with a relaxing bowl of tobacco as I watch the sky turn to red and dusk begin to settle on the mountaintop.

Berrypicking in this style grows on you, and I look forward to my annual trip as almost a pageant, a combination of scenic wilderness camping, meaningful economic activity, and the carrying forth of tradition. Odd though it may seem, I've never experienced boredom, in three days thus spent, comparable to that which I used to feel during those twenty minutes of berrypicking squeezed in as the incidental by-product of a day trip. With time, the simple, useful task of foraging for wild fruit becomes almost meditational; the fingers learn to do the bulk of work, the eyes are set free to relax, and the mind is released to wander at will.

At the end of my labors amongst the berrybushes, I always perform a little rite to mark the conclusion of my time on the mountain: Until this moment, excepting only a modest allotment of berries to sweeten my breakfast cereal, virtually every berry I've picked has gone "in [the] bucket, not in [my] mouth," happily as a result of self-discipline rather than the kind imposed from without. But now, with the last container

Berrypicking Days

Beneath the pepperidge and pine
The berries yet grow sweet and fine,
Thick as grapes upon the vine
Just as in days gone by.

No use to see them go to waste,
So juicy blue and sweet to taste,
When they can flavor golden cakes
And huckleberry pie.

So come and join me if you will,
And we will let the mountain fill
Our buckets with "blue gold" that grows
Wherever you may gaze,

And as we follow with our pails
Along the cairn-marked pickers' trails,
Let's keep alive the olden tales
Of berrypicking days!

M.B.F.

filled, a heavily laden bush in front of me, and my hands not quite ready for the shock of going cold turkey, I fill the last remaining storage space left to me: Engorging my mouth with berries until my cheeks puff out, I resist all temptation to chew or swallow until finally the pressure is too great to bear. The sweet, juicy fruit enveloping my taste buds is a satisfying reward for three days of perseverance. After repeating this performance a few times until my thirst is quenched, I throw all semblance of civilized restraint to the winds, and, using my hand only to steady the branch, I proceed to eat berries directly off the twig as a wild creature might. Then and only then am I ready to end my three days' immersion in huckleberrydom, pack up my tent, and trek down the mountain with my load, another year gone by, another year's huckleberry harvest heading home to my freezer.

In many ways my most memorable berrypicking trip was the one I experienced my first year camping on the high, rocky plateau near the Five-Mile Post. I had discovered this spot the previous autumn when a friend and I had camped along the Stony Kill, midway between the falls and the Smiley Road crossing, and had spent the next day following atop the ledges that form the northwest wall of the Stony Kill ravine. Our walk had taken us across the Smiley Road and on into the uppermost reaches of the stream's watershed, when we spied a secondary escarpment set back some distance to the northwest of the one we'd been following. We ate lunch atop this lofty plateau. I determined to return soon, so impressed was I with the beauty of the place.

The next summer I obtained permission to leave my car overnight along Rock Haven Road and hiked in along the fire access that leads to the Smiley Road. Turning southeastward, I proceeded along the road to the Five-Mile Post in order to confirm the availability of water. After filling a gallon jug, I backtracked for three or four minutes, then climbed the ledges on my left, ultimately proceeding inland toward my destination.

The view from the overlook where I set up camp looks deep into the Badlands and far across the upper Stony Kill and

The Berrypicker

Whenever in these hills you roam
You're never really quite alone;
Wherever you may go
A berrypicker's gone before.

He must have wandered through this way,
His basket brimming blue that day—
Here stands the cairn he built to say
He might be back for more.

His spirit fills the mountain still.
You'll meet him on the misty hill,
You'll find him in the bushes
Of the thicket and the swale,

You'll know him everywhere you see
The stones left there for you and me:
His monuments, our legacy,
The cairn-marked pickers' trail.

M.B.F.

154

the Fly Brook to the mountain ridge that rises impressively above a long stretch of the Peters Kill, from Castle Point on the right all the way down to Minnewaska. Looking farther toward the northeast, the eye follows the steep descent of the Stony Kill and looks out across the valley to the Berkshires in the distance. Farther to the left rise the familiar blue domes of the Catskill Mountains.

I gathered my berries from the swale at the foot of the escarpment below my campsite, sometimes mixing in a handful or two of low-bush fruit from above, for good measure. Late in the afternoon, when my day's berrypicking was done, I'd make my way back across the barrens to meet the Smiley Road along its descent toward the Stony Kill. At the crossing, beneath the little cascade that flows over the rocks immediately below the road, I'd enjoy a shower, utilizing a length or two of tent pole to project the trickle of water outward from the brink of the falls.

Finally, on the afternoon of the third day, I was ready to depart with my harvest of berries. I decided to shoot an azimuth with my sighting compass, so as to pick up the Smiley Road just enough to the near side of the fire road to allow for a small margin of error. During the previous two days, though my conscious focus was on harvesting huckleberries, never far from my mind were thoughts of the berrypickers of yore who had wandered these same rocky heights and shady swales at a time in history that overlapped even with my own childhood. The odd rock cairn marking a detour around thickets, or giving access to or from some solitary outcrop, became an archaeological messenger, bringing mute greetings from these people of another generation with whom my life had become so curiously intertwined. My compass-determined course took me through a stretch of anonymous territory I'd never had reason to traverse before, and my senses were heightened by the adventure and mood of anticipation implicit in such a trek. As I proceeded northward under my heavy load, I felt an inkling of what Professor Leakey must have experienced in Olduvai, my eyes scanning the ground for the hint of prior occupation that I knew might await me at any turn or lie hidden from view beneath some bush or stone.

After gaining the Smiley Road I continued just past the entrance to the fire trail, attracted by the presence of water crossing the roadway at Polack Swamp. I was delighted and surprised by the volume of water here, which surpassed the flow of the upper Stony Kill at this dry season of the year. Removing my pack, I enjoyed a cooling sponge bath of sorts from water that once refreshed Polack Joe and his family, and I silently acknowledged the simple wisdom of the man's choice for a campsite. Unspectacular as this little discovery may seem, it constituted a fitting enough conclusion to my three days in the footsteps of the berrypickers, and I headed down the fire road toward Mary Crose's Mountain and my old Plymouth Duster in a mood of very considerable contentment.

Appendix

The Blue Gold of Shawangunk Mountain

Words and music copyright 1991 by Marc B. Fried (as part of an unpublished collection entitled "Shawangunk Mountain Folktunes"). All rights reserved.

1. (Music as indicated)
Carry me back to that time of long ago,
To the tarpaper shack all the old folks know,
To the life they lived, seeking high and low
The blue gold of Shawangunk Mountain.

2. (Music as indicated)
In those rocky wilds, there I'll always be,
There a hundred miles of the Earth you'll see,
Where a hundred years folks sought eagerly
The blue gold of Shawangunk Mountain.

3. (Music as indicated)
They wandered all through these hills and swales,
From a carpet of blue they would fill their pails,
They've told me their stories, they've told me the tales
Of the blue gold of Shawangunk Mountain.

4. (Music as indicated)
When the hour grew late back to camp they'd come,
Round the fire they sat when their work was done,
In the spirits they drank and the songs they've sung
Was the blue gold of Shawangunk Mountain.

5. (Eight bars instrumental: chord progression as in verse 2)

6. (Another eight bars instrumental: chords as in verse 3)

7. (Music as in verse 2)
Some came from near, just below the mountainside,
Some traveled here from afar and wide
To return each year to their camps beside
The blue gold of Shawangunk Mountain.

8. (Music as in verse 4)
The rattlin' snake and the ol' black bear,
The porcupine too and the snowshoe hare
Were their neighbors in the wild where
Grew the blue gold of Shawangunk Mountain.

9. (Music as in verse 3)
The summer sun that burned so hot,
The mountain fire racin' 'cross the mountaintop,
These were part of the life of those who got
The blue gold of Shawangunk Mountain.

10. (Music as indicated above)
The thunder shower and the cooling breeze,
The towhee singin' from the tupelo trees,
These were also their memories,
Gatherin' blue gold on Shawangunk Mountain.

11. (Eight bars instrumental: chord progression as in verse 3)

12. (Music as in verse 1, with ritard for the last two bars)
Oh, carry me back to that time of long ago,
To the tarpaper shack all the old folks know,
To the life they loved, seeking high and low
The blue gold of Shawangunk Mountain.

THE CATSKILL MOUNTAIN HOUSE
America's Grandest Hotel
by Roland Van Zandt

The classic study of the pursuit of the Romantic Ideal in America, personified in the birth, growth and fiery death of the nation's first mountain resort hotel, built in 1823 and perched "like the wish of a child on the very edge of an overhanging ledge of the mountains, commanding a view that was once the most famous in America." *"The Catskill Mountain House is the story of a love affair—love at first sight. Mr. Van Zandt follows the great days of the famous hostelry with pride and the days of its decay with heartbreak." (The New York Times)* 448 pages, 94 illustrations, 9 maps, paper, $19.95.

THROUGH A WOMAN'S EYE,
Pioneering Photographers in Rural Upstate,
by Diane Galusha.

Turn-of-the-century rural America as it was seen and experienced by three farmers' daughters who became pioneering photographers in the remote northwestern Catskill Mountains. They became the principal chroniclers of their communities, preserving for all time images of a bygone world, affording the modern viewer a window on the past through the unique perspective of a woman's eye. *The rediscovery of a lost chapter in the history of photography. (Daily Gazette)* 200 pages, 61 full page photographs, paper, $29.95.

THE OLD EAGLE-NESTER
The Lost Legends of the Catskills
by Doris West Brooks

Nominated for a national story-telling award, *The Old Eagle-Nester* combines fiction and legend with a "pinch of magic and a smidgen of witchcraft." *"A beautifully designed and illustrated book,"* said the *Hudson Valley Literary Supplement. Dutchess Magazine* proclaimed, *"This is wonderful stuff, some of it funny, some of it frightening, all of it entertaining."* 128 pages, illustrations, paper, $13.95.

THE MILL ON THE ROELIFF JANSEN KILL
by The Roeliff Jansen Historical Society

From its founding in 1743 by the Livingston family, through 250 years of Hudson Valley history, the story of the oldest operating commercial mill in New York State, a collaborative work by seven historians, was recognized by a joint legislative resolution by the Senate and Assembly of New York State commemorating this publication. 144 pages, 36 photographs, 2 maps, paper, $15.00.

CHRONICLES OF THE HUDSON
Three Centuries of Travel and Adventure
by Roland Van Zandt

From Robert Juet aboard the Half Moon in 1609, to Henry James's reflections as he viewed the Hudson through the windows of a steam engine train in 1905, Van Zandt captures 300 years of travelers' adventures and perspectives in this "journey through time." Hudson Riverkeeper John Cronin, in his introduction notes: *"Each generation born to the Hudson is entitled to its own journey of discovery. Roland Van Zandt's legacy to us is as a friend and tour guide on that journey."* 384 pages, 51 illustrations & maps, paper, $24.95.

KAATERSKILL
From the Catskill Mountain House to the Hudson River School
by the Mountain Top Historical Society

The legendary Kaaterskill—synonymous with scenic beauty; inspiration for Thomas Cole and the Hudson River School; the birthplace of American mountain resorts; immortalized by James Fenimore Cooper and William Cullen Bryant; and now the heart of the Catskill Park and Preserve— profiled from seven different perspectives by seven prominent authors. 120 pages, 30 illustrations, hiking map, paper, $13.95.

BIG HOLLOW, A Mountaintop History
by Elwood Hitchcock

An intimate portrait of an isolated mountain valley community that witnessed the changing fortunes of the Catskills in microcosm; from wilderness to a scattering of family farms, through the "grand hotel" era, to the modern day—a return to quiet farms and country retreats in the shadow of a decaying resort, all amid the splendor of a hiker's paradise of thousands of acres of forest preserve. *"If there is such a thing as 'living history,' Mr. Hitchcock and his book are it." (The Advocate)* 128 pages, 25 illustrations, paper, $14.95.

A CATSKILLS BOYHOOD
My Life Along the Hudson
by Philip H. DuBois

An octogenarian professor emeritus recalls a bucolic childhood growing up in one of the oldest villages along the banks of the Hudson River, watching the advent of the modern age as the horse and carriage gives way to the Model-T. *"This book is filled with fascinating tidbits of life in the early century." (Kingston Freeman)* 128 pages, illustrations, paper, $12.95.

MOUNTAINTOP & VALLEY
Greene County Folk Arts Today
by Field Horne

Forty-eight folk artists profiled and photographed - from quilters, fish net weavers and stone wall builders to the "cutting edge" of chain saw carvers. Artists profiled were selected for the dignity and quality that their art presents, and the resulting book was awarded the coveted Heritage Award from the Federation of Historic Services. 48 pages, 33 photographs, paper, $10.00.

BLACK · DOME

Books available from the publisher:
BLACK DOME PRESS CORP.
RR 1, Box 422
Hensonville, NY, 12439
Tel: 518 734-6357   Fax: 518 734-5802
Prices & availability subject to change.